CONFLICT, ACTION AND SUSPENSE

BY

WILLIAM NOBLE

WRITER'S DIGEST BOOKS

CINCINNATI, OHIO

Other fine Writer's Digest Books are available from your local bookstore or direct from the publisher.

Visit our Web site at www.writersdigest.com for information on more resources for writers.

07   06   05   04   7   6   5   4

Library of Congress Cataloging-in-Publication Data

Noble, William.
    Conflict, action, and suspense / by William Noble.
       p.   cm.
    Includes index.
    ISBN 0-89879-907-4 (pbk. : alk. paper)
    1. Fiction—Technique.   I. Title.
  PN3355.N629   1994
  808.3—dc20   93-32778
                                       CIP

Edited by Jack Heffron

For Laura June
and Robert Dudnick

ABOUT THE AUTHOR

William Noble has been writing for twenty-nine years and has authored or coauthored many books, including the highly praised *Bookbanning in America* as well as *The Psychiatric Fix, The Private Me, How to Live With Other People's Children* and *Three Rules for Writing a Novel.* His books for writers include several that have become main selections of the Writer's Digest Book Club: *Show Don't Tell, "Shut Up!" He Explained* and *Make That Scene, Steal This Plot.* His *The 28 Biggest Writing Blunders (And How to Avoid Them)* was published by Writer's Digest Books. His short fiction and nonfiction have appeared in more than forty periodicals.

When he began to write full time, he shed his career as a Pennsylvania attorney and never looked back. In addition to his books, stories and articles, he has taught or lectured about writing at the Breadloaf Writer's Conference, Imagination Writer's Conference, New England Young Writer's Conference, Northern Waters Writer's Conference, Goddard College, the Community College of Vermont and in public schools in Connecticut and Vermont.

He earned his J.D. from the University of Pennsylvania and his B.A. from Lehigh University, and while in college he worked in the CBS newsroom in New York and also wrote television scripts. He has appeared on numerous television and radio shows in connection with his writing and lives near the sea in a quiet village in New Jersey.

CONTENTS

INTRODUCTION

"Tell me a story!" is the not-so-private wish of every reader. "Make me care, excite me, scare me. . . . " and woe to the writer who doesn't get the message.

Readers may seek us out for enlightenment or for intellectual give and take, but above all they want a story that will transport them beyond the curtain of their own reality. They yearn for clues that reveal something of themselves so they can become involved. They want to *participate* in the happenings on the page, and the careful writer understands a story must allow this to happen. What it comes to is this: Reader and writer are partners, understanding one another's needs and aware of one another's expectations so the finished product satisfies both. Writers expect readers to stay glued to the story . . . but readers expect writers to fashion a story to which they can stay glued. Each has obligations to the other, and the value of the finished product will show how well those obligations have been shouldered.

This book works from the premise that the writer-reader partnership offers value and that no story develops well without the writer's awareness that the partnership is ongoing and demanding. Writers who ignore their readers' expectations do so at their own peril, and readers who dismiss their writer's technical craft miss story significance. *Appreciate your reader!* might be an appropriate commandment for all writers . . . but readers should be equally urged to *appreciate your writer!*

Partnership, you see.

What I've tried to do is examine conflict, action and suspense against the background of writer-reader partnership. We can't develop good stories without thinking of the reader and understanding the effects of what we've written. Conflict, for example, only works when we appreciate that the reader will be moved by it, and we should know that in the writer-reader partnership it is the *reader's* reaction we strive for.

Conflict is key in all forms of story writing but especially with action and suspense. Conflict means drama, and no story of action or suspense will work well without drama. Throughout this book I emphasize how drama must be portrayed if action and suspense are to flow. But what I really mean is that conflict should be honed so it can turn sluggish drama into something highly charged. There are different types of conflict, of course — it can be subtle as well as overt, or threatening as well as comedic. But for a good story to emerge, the conflict must be clear and unambiguous. We must *know* who or what is pitted against whom or what, and we must understand the consequences.

For conflict is really a mechanism that sparks all stories, and in this book we'll see how it builds action and suspense. There are no stories of conflict *per se*; that is, all stories use conflict to develop themselves, to fan excitement, and to create drama and the ultimate climax. We'll see how all that can be accomplished.

Though this book will usually couple action and suspense, there are obvious differences in their story effect. Here's a short-hand rubric:

- Action means happenings.
- Suspense means uncertainty.

When we write an action scene, we must understand that it's going to involve a "happening," something done, physical or mental exertion. Action scenes are not contemplative.

When we write a suspense scene, we must see it as a build-up of uncertainty, keeping the reader guessing and leaving question marks. Suspense scenes may be contemplative, though they don't have to be.

Often there can be both action and suspense in the same story (see Peter Benchley's *Jaws* [Doubleday] or Herman Melville's *Moby Dick* for widely varied possibilities). When we examine story openings and endings, or how we build through mood and atmosphere, or any of the other chapter material, we see that most of the techniques work equally well with either action or suspense.

Yet throughout the book, the differences between action and suspense are highlighted, especially when they might relate to individual scenes or sketches. Sometimes the way to develop an action scene is *not* the way to develop a suspense scene, and we'll see why. Action, after all, is more direct and more immediate than suspense, which thrives on indirectness and the hope of a payoff somewhere down the line. Action throbs while suspense quivers; action shouts while suspense whispers; action does while suspense hints. . . .

We'll see how it works and how *you* can make it work, too.

CHAPTER 1

THE NUTS AND BOLTS OF DRAMA

WHAT MAKES A STORY interesting? What holds a reader's attention? What rivets eyes to the page and feeds an urge for more and more and more?

It isn't fuscia-colored ink or exquisite calligraphy or richly textured paper.

It's *drama*—taking facts and making them live, developing characters so they become memorable. We sculpt and we hone and we recast so a pedestrian set of circumstances can become interesting, even exciting, even . . . breathtaking.

Drama is what we seek to create because drama is a wand that can turn boring events into attention-grabbers, and when this happens on the written page, we'll find a reader involved in the story and thirsting for more.

Consider: A young man takes a journey to see an old aunt

- who offers nothing but complaints.
- who tells him his father was illegitimate.

A stream of complaints may develop insight into the character, may even add to story background, but it's not what a reader will find enticing in long doses. A careful writer might be able to sneak in a gem of plot enhancement among the complaints, but it requires subtlety and gentle-fingered control, something less experienced writers have difficulty with. For the most part, a stream of complaints pushes the reader back from the developing story because they leave a bad taste. No one (well, almost no one) finds that appealing, and the result dampens drama and punctures interest.

But what of the second event? Here's something *dramatic*! Illegitimacy, not of a friend, not of a character in the newspaper, but yours, his, mine! A shock—unexpected, unnerving and unadorned. Naked truth, but with a kicker.

The reason: It's interesting. That's what drama does: It heightens interest and charges the atmosphere. Suppose *we* find out, suddenly, that our father was illegitimate, that the family line we had confidently assumed to be unbroken was never there? We'd want to know why and how and when and we'd want to know *right away*.

And so will the reader. A sense of drama powers action and suspense stories because they rely on an upsurge of reader involvement, and the clearest way to provide the drama is to have something happen.

But even before we have drama, we must have conflict. It is the essence of story development, and whether we call it *tension*, *discord*, or a host of other synonyms, it means, simply, that the story contains someone or something struggling with someone or something and the outcome is in doubt. Conflict creates drama, and it establishes the focus of the action or the suspense to follow. Then, we portray an event, an incident, a circumstance, a surprise, something that will break up the cool tone and jar the reader's complacency. That's dramatic impact, and that's where action and suspense blossom. The event can be as subtle as a change in wind direction or as blatant as a volcanic eruption, but the key is to produce a happening, because this will keep the reader's attention, which has already been tuned in by the conflict.

Think of that old schooltime activity "Show and Tell." Drama is showing, and the best way to bring it out is by creating an incident, a happening. Which is more effective . . . to describe a boy's lengthy walk to grandmother's house or to have him *run* to grandmother's because he saw a ghost in the forest? Obviously the latter, because the incident (seeing the ghost in the forest) charges the prose and makes it spark. There's conflict and there's action, and the reader wants to make sure the boy will reach grandmother's safely.

There may well be a time, of course, when an incident-free walk to grandmother's suits the purpose of the story (perhaps the boy is wrestling with a major decision). Action *on the walk* is not necessary. But to build drama, we should have an incident and we should be able to show it.

THE NEED FOR CONFRONTATION

"All happy families resemble one another," wrote Leo Tolstoy in *Anna Karenina*, "every unhappy family is unhappy in its own way." Many of us are familiar with this observation, though we've reworked it a time or two to suit our own storytelling. But it states the essence of dramatic purpose. Let's paraphrase: Happy families are alike, unhappy families are different. Or put another way:

- Happy families are dull.
- Unhappy families are interesting.

Why the difference? It's the distinction between losing yourself in a crowd and maintaining individuality, between wearing a common blue uniform and wearing the only red uniform on the field. All eyes focus on the red uniform, but who can find you in the crowd when everyone is wearing the same blue color?

Drama seeks to bring the unusual, the unexpected to the reader's attention, just as the red uniform will bring you to the attention of the crowd. But that's only part of the struggle because now we have to hold onto the attention we've worked so hard to grab, and that's where Leo Tolstoy's message rings bright and clear — "Every unhappy family is unhappy in its own way."

Unhappy is the operative word now. We've established the family as unusual (the red uniform, so to speak), but to keep the reader's attention we have to develop that family. And the key is to understand that there must be *confrontation*, a struggle of some sort. Isn't that part of the mix in an unhappy family? Un-happiness breeds confrontation, and that's why Tolstoy's comment is right on the money.

Because confrontation is drama. It is an incident, a showing, not a telling. There is a dramatic story in every unhappy family.

> If only I'd known the depths of mother's grief over Charles' death, I would never have tried to re-create his paintings. I thought she needed cheering up when what she wanted was oblivion.

Imagine the confrontation that would have taken place here when the narrator tried to re-create the paintings, and you get a sense of the dramatic impact. If this was a happy family, such a scene would probably not have happened. But the unhappy family forms the foundation for the confrontation, which becomes an incident, which then becomes drama.

Confrontation, of course, is merely another way of referring to conflict, though it implies a more narrow base. Confrontation is certainly conflict, but conflict is more than confrontation (e.g., two characters may have conflicting goals, but they may never confront one another). Yet confrontation, *any* confrontation, will get the reader's attention, and if it's portrayed vividly enough, that attention will not waver.

Conflict in the form of confrontation comes in various ways: between the characters themselves (a rivalry or a chase), between characters and their environment (a struggle to survive on the open sea), or between characters and themselves (a struggle to overcome the effects of a debilitating injury or phobia). A confrontation that falls into one or more of these categories (one or more because there can be different kinds of confrontation within the same story, even with the same character) is the way we begin to develop action and suspense.

Imagine a saga set on a lush Caribbean island. The sultry environment is a perfect foil for disquieting circumstances such as terror, murder or intrigue. Could any of these happen if there is no confrontation at some level? Something or someone has to set terror in motion, and when the perpetrator meets the victim (as will surely happen), there is a confrontation.

> "Three drops from this bottle, and the water system goes pffffft," the strange old man cackled.
> Jim and I looked at one another with rising despair. The ankle chains kept us hobbled and impotent.

The action springs from this confrontation, and the story moves forward with drama. The nature of the confrontation develops the "showing" that we hope to achieve because now we can picture the scene. It's the confrontation that allows it to happen, and we stay interested.

Why? Well, the accomplished writer knows that the best way to gain the reader's attention is by offering the reader a chance to root for one of the characters, allowing the reader to take sides. Developing a confrontation creates a rooting opportunity because there are, of course, two sides (maybe more, actually), and someone has to win. Making the confrontation vivid enough (*dramatic!*) provides the reader the chance to jump in and root.

And that's how you hook 'em.

PULL ON THOSE EMOTIONS

Once I had a writing student who took issue with a comment I made on his story. "These characters are dull," I wrote. "The reader doesn't get interested in them."

"I researched this a lot," he said. "You always told us to know our characters."

"They're flat," I said. "Your research hasn't helped to make them interesting."

"Well, I wasn't looking for that."

But that's exactly what he should have been looking for . . . and writing about. Whether it's characterization or plot or general story approach, we must search out the interesting elements and let the reader chew on them. A story is not a lecture or an academic treatise, it's supposed to be exciting, attention-grabbing; if we wipe away the interesting parts, we've lost the primary reason for the story's existence.

One way we excite the reader is to portray strong emotions and give the reader a chance to feel them. The stronger the emotion, the more the reader can jump in. Think of anger. Modest annoyance might not even generate reaction from a character (nor cause the reader to have anything but a ho-hum response), but where the character *explodes, vibrates, roars, fumes, erupts*, the reader can feel the tingle and sense the cloud of emotion that bursts from the page. This type of anger is strong indeed, and few readers would be immune. Strong emotions, developed through sharp conflict, are necessary to build and maintain the drama. The reader *feels* the consequences.

Take Stephen King, for example. Suspense and horror flow through his stories with syrupy ease. Ordinary things don't happen to his characters; ordinary events don't take place in his story settings. And his characters don't react in modest ways. Their emotions surge. This is how drama develops, and it brings life to even the most innocuous of circumstances. In *Misery* (Viking), a well-known writer, Paul Sheldon, is injured in a car accident in a remote area of Colorado and is rescued by Annie Wilkes, who turns out to be his most obsessive fan. She takes him to her house and slowly nurses him back to health, all the while slipping him Novril, a painkiller, and growing more and more possessive. Gradually, he begins to realize his predicament.

> He discovered three things almost simultaneously, about ten days after having emerged from the dark cloud. The first was that Annie Wilkes had a great deal of Novril (she had, in fact a great many drugs of all kinds). The second was that he was hooked on Novril. The third was that Annie Wilkes was dangerously crazy.

End of chapter. But what a legacy the author leaves! Deep-rooted fear, a character's life at risk. These are the story tenacles the author dangles, and the reader will be caught in them. The emotions are strong, the reader develops fears along with the character, and how can anyone stay aloof from the story? What's happened is that drama has burst out because strong emotions have been portrayed. Strong emotions *mean* drama. All of us have memories of dramatic incidents in our lives; how many times have they *not* been accompanied by strong emotions? And that's what's happened here. We get involved in the story because of the strong emotions the author has brought in, and in a tale of suspense like this the emotional level is crucial.

Sometimes a series of special details might add to the excitement because it provides an opportunity to round out the mental picture the reader should take away. Which is more enticing?

The dirt track vibrated with vehicles chasing one another round and round, first one gaining the lead, then another. . . .

or

Noise and smoke and whoop-it-up crowds pushed the evening's soft air beyond the concrete stadium shell, and peacock-colored blurs sped around the dirt oval like electrons around a nucleus in a kaleidoscopic light show.

Details, details. Obviously, I've added some image-provoking language in the second selection, but even so, it offers more details (crowds and smoke and noise and concrete stadium and soft air and a dirt oval and vehicle colors) than the first selection. Note how the picture is so much clearer and fuller; the reader can grasp the circumstances more easily and feel more involved.

The reason? The reader knows more because the details are provided. To know more is to *feel* more.

D.H. Lawrence was especially good at using carefully crafted details because he knew they offered strong dramatic impact. Details can create emotional upsurge. Take a look at this description of a wooded glen in *Lady Chatterley's Lover*, the day after Connie Chatterley and the gamekeeper make love for the first time. Note the surging emotion in Connie:

It was a grey, still afternoon, with the dark-green dog's-mercury spreading under the hazel copse, and all the trees making a silent effort to open their buds. Today she could almost feel it in her own body, the huge heaves of the sap in the massive trees, upwards, up, up to the bud-tips, there to push into little flamey oak-leaves, bronze as blood.

In his use of details, Lawrence has injected emotion, and we can sense the tingling awareness in the character as she contemplates her feelings for her new lover. Lawrence could have written that she stood in the woods and thought about the gamekeeper, but instead, he writes that she becomes one of the massive trees and *feels* those things the trees must be feeling. This is emotional reaching out by means of detail development, and the reader would be hard pressed to avoid becoming involved.

ESCALATE, ESCALATE

A crucial part of any action or suspense writing is to keep the reader's attention at a high level. The problem is that a constant dose of conflict will eventually cause the reader to yawn at the sameness of it all. It's like the first time we eat caviar: exciting, delectable, all those happy sensations. But if we eat it the next day and the next and the next, for an entire month, the allure wanes, and pretty soon we're screaming for something else. Anything!

It's the same in story writing; we have to keep control of our action and suspense sequences so they don't overwhelm the reader and turn exciting scenes into drab replays. Drama, of course, relies on conflict, but it should build or change rather than remain constant. Don't, for example, begin with the most severe action sequence in the book. Don't try to show the most riveting conflict in the earliest stages (although your first scene must be strong enough to hook the reader). Save the best for last. Build up to the severest action, the most riveting conflict.

In other words, escalate your conflict. Have the drama build to a natural climax. Otherwise, you risk running a race and leading for a while, only to find the other runners passing you on the backstretch and pulling farther and farther ahead. Drama must build; it cannot stay at a constant level.

How do we escalate? First, we try not to overwhelm the reader in the early stages. If, for example, the climax is a well-planned murder, we cause problems for ourselves if the protagonist (or protagonists) divulge early in the story how they will commit the crime. Where can we escalate from there? The drama level is already high.

Or if the climax is an athletic success, we hurt our story by having a similiar success early in the story (unless, of course, the protagonist has been injured, and now must try and regain some lost glory in the face of the injury, but here, at least, we've started the story over again, and the protagonist must escalate new successes to the final one). Once we lose that subtle aura of drama, it's extremely hard to regain it.

One way to escalate is to keep adding uncertainties to a resolution of the conflict. For example, a passion for revenge might become complicated by a love interest (call this the *Romeo and Juliet* factor), or it might expand to more individuals, or it might create some return revenge so the hunter becomes the hunted. All of these circumstances are possible, but with each additional piece of baggage, we've increased the level of drama and added to dramatic possibilities. See how Elmore Leonard does it in *Glitz* (Arbor House), a novel that flows between Puerto Rico and Atlantic City. It's a story of revenge as Teddy Magyk, a psychopathic killer, stalks Vincent Mora, a policeman who put him in prison some years before.

Initially, they have a confrontation (read, conflict) in Puerto Rico, where Vincent has been recuperating from on-the-job injuries. Teddy is hustled off the island by a couple of Vincent's friends before he can do damage to Vincent, and that seems to settle things (at least in Vincent's mind). But Elmore Leonard has other ideas, and he begins to add uncertainties and complications, escalating the suspense and the action.

First, he has a Puerto Rican friend (female) of Vincent's move to Atlantic City to try to make herself some big money; then he has Teddy show up in Atlantic City (because his mother lives there) and discover Vincent's friend. Teddy toys with her before he brutally kills her, knowing that this will bring Vincent to Atlantic City, unaware Teddy is waiting for him. Now, matters escalate to a high level because Vincent is searching for the unknown killer of his friend, while Teddy is watching Vincent and waiting for his opportunity—each, in effect, is stalking the other, and the tension climbs. Finally, Teddy kills an elderly tourist because he needs money, and the brutal way he commits the crime rings bells in Vincent's head:

> He could see Teddy at his trial almost eight years before, and a stout woman with blond hair in the first row. Vincent did tell himself he was dealing with a remote possibility at best. Because if Teddy's presence is so logical now, why hadn't he thought of Teddy before this? And his gut feeling would say, Never mind that. He's here.

Now, each is aware of the other. Story conflict has reached that pure stage where there's no doubt about motive or identity. Each character knows who he is after and why.

And the story has escalated far beyond its early level when Teddy's menace for Vincent was vague and fairly low key, and Vincent's menace for Teddy was more talk than action. But the more familiar we become with Teddy, the more vicious he becomes, and the more familiar we become with Vincent, the more determined he becomes. The conflict sparks . . . then flames . . . then explodes!

That's escalation, folks.

IMMEDIACY DOES THE TRICK

Nothing we ever write can match the dramatic impact of an event or circumstance that happens *now, this instant, here!* We're excited by the present because that's where our lives pulse and breathe. We see things most clearly when they happen *today!*

And the impact on us is keenest because we can reach out and touch reality. That doesn't mean we couldn't get caught up in story drama taking place in the past or future; many successful writers connect with readers regardless of the time setting. But today's drama gives us a special boost because it's happening before our eyes!

We call this *immediacy* because the story unfolds while we watch, and the drama touches us with its contemporary spontaneity. We are in the immediate presence of what is happening.

Writers have long known how to develop a sense of immediacy so it can have maximum impact on the reader, so it can bring the reader face to face with drama at a high level. Obviously, we must start with a tale that reflects what is happening around us, something contemporary with dramatic possibilities. A new technology, perhaps, or a social upheaval or even a political assassination. It must register on our readers that the story fits right between the lines of the morning newspaper, or springs from the nightly television screen. It must shout, "This is what's happening *today!* You've read about it, you've watched it unfold." Because it's so touchable, readers will feel that they're a part of the story and will be able to balance themselves on familiar ground.

We have the techno-thriller, for example, which offers a pure sense of immediacy. Any story that wraps itself around highly sophisticated, breathtakingly accomplished equipment and uses esoteric designations to make it more mysterious provides a science fiction allure:

> The XT channel selector had its electronic pulse spray magnesium particles on the cam of the Alpha-Two listening device so voice inflections could be remagnetized and woven into the titanium-powered word box of the RL-7 robot.

This, of course, is nothing but my imagination at work, but it shows how intriguing we could get with techno-talk and the use of mind-stretching equipment. Pick up a newspaper and read a story of a space launch or scan a piece about new computer usage or military weapon development, and there will be some techno-talk. We won't understand all the descriptions, nor will we (probably) think to ask what the esoteric numbers stand for. But the writers of techno-thrillers do understand, because they do prodigious research to ensure the accuracy their readers' demand.

We'll nod with some degree of certainty that this techno-talk must be describing a remarkable piece of equipment, and anyway, other people are paid to know how all of this works. It must be important if it does the things it's supposed to do.

When we add elements of conflict and weave them into action and suspense scenes, we have the techno-thriller, and a host of writers (such as Tom Clancy and Dale Brown) have lit a fire to the market. By combining today's exciting technology with drama-producing techniques, we develop a story that's as immediate as the next page you'll turn (after you finish this page, of course).

Actually, any contemporary story circumstance will do the trick (the techno-thriller is only one type). Serial murders, right now, are big, as is financial manipulation in the U.S. Government's budget mess. These topics (and many others, too) are what's happening *today* and their immediacy provides a foundation for drama, which can then develop the action and suspense.

Using name brands is another way of bringing immediacy to your story. Product references can catch the reader's attention, and if we use several names in a few short sentences, the hook will be well placed:

> He bunched the Golden Arches throwaway and heaved it toward the idling 450 SL, knowing his fawn gray Pierre Cardin suit ran the risk of muddy retaliation.

Obviously, this can be overdone. You shouldn't name-brand everything, but a judicious sprinkling of current product or place names will bring things into closer perspective for the reader, and the sense of immediacy will grow. We identify with name brands, and the reader will, too.

We get the same kind of effect when we focus on the feelings and reactions of the characters. The more we develop those feelings, the more the reader will become involved in what happens. Instead of writing "Mary shed tears," think more comprehensively about how Mary must have felt and what went through her head. Then, we could write, "Mary remembered an earlier time, on a playground somewhere, a little boy falling and lying inert, the groping terror that sprung tears to her eyes. Would he get up, would he *breathe* again?" It's people—characters—who are the most important elements in a story, and the more interesting we make them, the easier it will be for readers to feel a part of the story. Delve into their feelings—sadness, greed, fury, orderliness—show us why the feelings are there and how they will influence later actions or other feelings. Try to make the characters "live" on the page, because this is how we create the "now" world, which is a strong scene-setter for dramatic portrayal.

The sense of immediacy can burst forth from many sources, but the important thing to remember is that its effect can be drama-producing, because it uses conflict to thrust the reader into action and suspense sequences that are right there, on the morning news or in the daily newspaper. The reader's fiction world and the real world become one and the same.

CHAPTER 2

STAGE-SETTING

GOOD WRITING IS MUCH MORE than a tap on our imaginations. If imagination was all we used, we'd end up with anarchic prose because we'd have no way to turn a fountain of ideas into a stream of story. Writing *technique* is what we must master, taking ideas and molding them into something readers can identify with and enjoy. We're all familiar with the cliché, "writing is 10 percent talent, 90 percent hard work." Well, the hard work is the application of techniques to turn ideas into story. Talent comes with imagination, but the hard work comes in using it effectively.

To create and sustain action and suspense, the story line should be bold and solid. For example, one character could be conversing with another, knowing the other is a vicious killer, but trying not to show that knowledge. It could be underplayed by matter-of-fact dialogue, or it could be overdramatized by highly charged nervousness. Either way, the conflict in the scene would be heightened by *how* the author dramatized it—the techniques used to underplay or overplay. Technique in a situation like this becomes a procedural device for turning the action and suspense into something the reader doesn't want to pull away from.

As we'll see, procedural devices include grammar techniques, image-provoking language and stage direction to energize the story so the action and suspense build. Some stories, of course, need little assistance from procedural applications because they are inherently so suspenseful and dramatic. Think of Edgar Allan Poe's "The Tell-Tale Heart." Such unrelieved suspense doesn't need special effects to make it more involving; it is a riveting story of a murderer and a victim and suspicious visitors. Even if the story was one unbroken narrative, a single paragraph from end to end, it would still be consuming. The story, itself, needs no special dramatic effect, but this is, by far, the exception. Most stories benefit from procedural devices that bolster the effects they reach for, and this is not to minimize these stories in the least. The chance of coming up with "The Telltale Heart" is rare enough, so none of us would accomplish much by waiting to develop it in our imaginations. Better to conjure up a story we like and see if we can build the action and suspense and conflict by using procedural techniques.

I call this *stage-setting* because these devices become the props that allow the story to move along the path we wish. If it's an action story, then we know certain devices will help to develop the action—at least in the reader's mind—and we rely upon them to do that. If it's a suspense story, we understand what we can do to ratchet the suspense up or down, page by page, paragraph by paragraph, even word by word. It has little to do with the story line itself, but much to do with *the way* the story is told.

We set the stage, and the story takes it from there.

IT BEGINS WITH GRAMMAR

It's pretty well acknowledged that readers "hear" as well as see words on the page. That is, word sounds and word images play in the readers' minds even as their eyes scan the words. Some have referred to this as "the music of words," others as an appeal to "word-sense," but the important thing is to understand that the way words "sound" on the page will affect what the reader takes away. Much of it has to do with—ugh!—grammar: The tense, the voice, the sentence structure and paragraphing we develop will influence the word-music the reader "hears."

Consider:

The flames licked closer and closer, and he shuddered with the certainty he would die.

or

The certainty of death was making him shudder, and his space was being licked closer and closer by the flames.

In trying to build action or suspense, which of these works better? Obviously the first selection, and the reason is that it uses the *active* voice, which charges the story and gives it life. The passive voice, used in the second selection, simply doesn't do this. The active voice with its direct and straightforward verb use rivets our attention. When we want to move things along, this is what we reach for so the story pace won't slip. Therefore, it's

- Frank turned the wheel, *not* the wheel was turned by Frank.
- Mary shouted at the boat, *not* the boat was being shouted at by Mary.
- The door squeaked open, *not* squeaky sounds were being made by the door as it opened.

This is not to say the passive voice doesn't have a place; of course it does, but that place is limited in stories in which action and suspense occur. The passive voice works best to change the pace, to stretch and extend narrative, or to diminish emphasis on action and suspense. But it's the active voice for active stories.

It's the same with paragraphing and sentence structure. To speed things along, we want to have shorter, snappier sentences; clipped paragraphs; sharp transitions. We want the story to *move*, and lengthy sentences or long, unbroken paragraphs have the effect of inducing a more leisurely style (which might work as a change of pace, but not as a general approach).

Suppose, for example, we have a character searching for documents in a house where the occupants might return at any time. It's a tense situation, and if we use long sentences and lengthy paragraphs, we tend to reduce the drama and tenseness. See how it could work:

> Ah, a recessed drawer. Not locked even. Who'd suspect him here tonight, anyway?
> Maybe the documents are gone.
> She said she saw them. All right, trust her, for now.
> The drawer's stuck. Don't break it. . . .

Note how the quick pace builds the action (and establishes conflict), which, of course, is what we seek to accomplish. Writers as diverse as Ernest Hemingway and James Joyce used this technique when they wanted to speed things up, because they understood that the reader would "hear" the quickened pace as well as see it.

Suppose we want to depict one person's growing awareness of another's murderous intentions. Do we write a lengthy description?

> It wasn't the words so much as the tone of voice where he bit off his anger and seemed to hiss as he mentioned her name, and then his face grew black hard in the early light, and I began to understand why we'd come to this empty place where the city glowed in the distance.

Or do we shorten things?

> The tone of voice rattled me. Not the words. Anger, anger was in his mind! At her, of course, hissing her name, her failure to love him. Black hard fury crossed his face. The early light made things clear. An empty place at the city's edge. . . .

Which example builds suspense more? Obviously, the second because of the shorter sentences, a rat-tat-tat that quickens the reader's pulse and the action in the story. The "music" the reader hears isn't a melodic rhapsody, it's up-tempo jazz.

We get the same effect when we use verbs that stimulate this word-music. The bell didn't "ring," it "clanged." The sludge didn't "drip," it "oozed." The air didn't "sweeten," it "sugar-blossomed."

Two things at work here: Just as with the active voice, we must try to stay with active verbs. (My dictionary distinguishes active and passive verbs this way: Active means the *performance* of action, passive means the *endurance* of action). So,

- He hurt, *not* he suffered.
- She wrote, *not* she was written about.

Also, we must try to use active verbs that will spark the word-music for the reader. The train can speed, but it can also *churn*; the eyes can follow, but they can also *devour*. We have to think in images (more about this in the next section) because imagery is what blossoms in the readers' minds when they absorb words from the page. An *image-creating* active verb is what we seek, and this will have the effect of boosting both the action and the suspense. Here's Joseph Conrad in *The End of the Tether* describing horses and carriages on a sea road in a Far Eastern port:

> The bright domes of the parasols swayed lightly outwards like full-blown blossoms on the rim of a vase; and the quiet sheet of dark-blue water, crossed by a bar of purple, made a background for the spinning wheels and the high action of the horses, whilst the turbaned heads of the Indian servants elevated above the line of the sea horizon glided rapidly on the paler blue of the sky.

The parasols *swayed*, the turbaned heads *glided*. These are image-provoking active verbs, and we get a mental picture of the scene. It keeps us in close touch with the story and with what's going on.

CHARGE UP THOSE IMAGES

One day a friend asked if I would read some material an acquaintance had left with her. "She wants to write," my friend said. The acquaintance had recently retired from middle management and decided her next career would be as a writer.

"She's sure she has talent," my friend added.

Inwardly I groaned because I knew that writing isn't something a person "picks up" at a convenient stage in life. It's a passion that gnaws at the soul from an early age. But I said I'd look over the material since my friend was sure there was good writing here. "She always had good grades in school," my friend remembered.

It didn't take long to realize that the work, which included poems, a short story, a television play and literary criticism, had little, if any, chance of being published. It wasn't the subject matter and it wasn't the effort. She had been serious about what she had done, and she had been able to see story possibilities in a number of ideas.

The problem was the writing had turned out to be dull, dull, dull. She had not developed the drama in her stories, she had left the reader in the cold—uninvolved. She had not allowed the reader to *feel* what was happening.

In short, she did not *appeal* to the reader's heart.

"I feel, therefore I am," is a wise goal, and an experienced writer knows this is the clearest way to get readers involved. Make them care!

Use charged images. Make the mental picture life-size!

My friend's acquaintance didn't do this. Instead of "bursting in blossomy harness," she wrote "opening like a flower." Instead of "daubs on my electric canvas," she wrote "tidbits of my life." She stayed with recognizable, often-used—and dull—phrases, such as:

- "every rustle of a leaf, or snap of a twig"
- "distinctive fragrance"
- "lulls you to sleep"

She might have been accurate, but she wasn't dramatic, and she wasn't imaginative.

Charging your images produces feeling in the reader and that feeling then involves the reader. Think excitement and bursting emotion: The engine *roared*, the woman *radiated*, the ship *bucked* and *wallowed*.

Especially in action stories the use of charged images add excitement because they expand the reader's awareness of what is happening. Which is more interesting to read about: "a large, ugly man" or "a monstrous, moon-faced jailkeeper"?

We charge the image by using adjectives and nouns and verbs that convey a particular mental picture. The narrower and more focused we make that picture, the more it will take shape and project in the reader's mind. Aaron Elkins, in the 1987 Edgar Award-winning mystery *Old Bones* (Mysterious Press), describes a man marooned by an incoming tide in Mont-Saint-Michel Bay, France:

> With dismay the old man watched the arm of water through which he plodded swell and send out tendrils of its own.

We get a more developed picture with this description than if he had written that the water was rising and spreading. Elkins shows us the water has an arm and is able to send out tendrils. He personifies the water, and in doing this he creates a scene and charges the image.

The key to much of this is to avoid falling back on clichés, which my friend's friend was unable to do. Of course leaves rustle, of course twigs snap, of course something will have a distinctive fragrance, but there's nothing new in that.

We need to share a different feeling, something unusual, not expected. When we read that leaves rustle, it doesn't impress us much because we've read it or heard it so many times that it has little significance. Even the most bizarre event can become uninteresting if we're exposed to it enough. (Imagine the mortician's blasé manner as he prepares a body for viewing.) Rustling leaves are what we expect, and so they don't charge the image. But if the leaves *quiver* or *shrivel*, then, the image blossoms.

And no one thinks of clichés.

In many stories, some menace stalks the characters or comprises a great challenge. It might be inanimate, such as a desert or great forest the characters must endure, or it might be an individual or group of individuals that must be faced down.

Here, of course, is the essence of conflict because the menace represents the antagonistic force that creates the story's drama, and conflict is the underpinning of drama. The menace becomes more image-charged when we portray it in larger-than-life form. For instance:

- a storm becomes a *violent hurricane*.
- a criminal is *seven feet tall*, has *six fingers on a hand*, or is *overwhelmingly bloodthirsty*.
- a virus can mutate into *population-destroying form*.

When we depict any of these images, the menace develops into an intolerable threat ("bigger than life"), and once that happens, the reader's imagination is on high hum. In action and suspense, events and personalities like these set up conflict, which creates imagery that becomes a vibrant stage for all that will follow.

SHIFT THAT POINT OF VIEW

One concept that befuddles inexperienced writers is the notion of "point of view," or as the late editor William Sloane described it, "the means of perception." Time and again there is collective head scratching over the difference between subjective and objective approaches and between first-person and third-person characterizations (with an occasional second-person variation that, unfortunately, does complicate things). *I saw the man climb the tree* is first-person subjective. *He saw the man climb the tree* is third-person objective.

The personal pronoun we use—*I* or *you* or *he* or *she*—defines what the character is capable of sensing or knowing or acquiring. The character's "means of perception" limits or expands the nature of the story. If, for example, we write a first-person story, everything the lead character does or thinks must be limited by what that character can perceive—events and conversations taking place "offstage," so to speak, would not be known because the character didn't see or hear them. The story, or at least the scene, remains believable only if we adhere to this—the point of view must stay constant.

But if we use the third person (and sometimes the second person), we can expand the story line because the writer becomes omnniscient. The writer can skip around and have things happening to or dialogue developing between several characters and at several locations. The writer becomes a chessmaster, moving characters around to build the game, unconstrained by the limitations of a first-person subjective approach. The writer sees all, and the characters are his pawns! The point of view is objective because the writer sits above the characters instead of settling inside them.

Essentially, these are the distinctions in the concept of point of view—where does the writer sit when developing the story? Inside the characters? Outside the characters? It makes a difference.

Preparing most stories demands that we nail down our point of view, early, early, early. How the story moves along depends on this because we'll need to know right off what the characters are capable of sensing or not sensing, knowing or not knowing. So we must plan carefully, and this becomes another way of stage-setting. This is the truest application of *how* we intend to write the story.

Then, because we're working with action and suspense, we know we can manipulate our point of view in order to juice up story pace. We can flip between characters in such a way that the reader knows we're inside each of them at the time we have them speak or think or act. Tom Clancy is especially good at this. Take a look at some of his novels, *The Hunt for Red October* (Naval Institute Press) and *The Sum of All Fears* (Putnam), for example. Note how he shifts scenes and chapters, some less than a page in length, once in a while only a few lines long. Note, too, that with many shifts the point of view changes, sometimes the change covers thousands of miles and different continents.

By doing this, Clancy ratchets up the pace of the story, causing the reader to jump with him in order to stay abreast of the action. Quick scene cuts are especially appropriate in the fiction we're discussing because each time we make a sharp shift in point of view, the tension rises, and when we make these shifts at short intervals, the tension spurs the action and the suspense. For example:

> . . . and he didn't want to think what was behind the steel door.

and

> She knew he stood but a few feet away, only the solid door separated them. But did he know she was there?

and

> He wanted to walk away before the agony in the next room could claim him. His life meant nothing now, he'd lost all interest when she'd been taken.

His to hers and back to his, we could carry this on for a while, shifting points of view and moving the action on—two characters in the same place involved in the same action, yet having different reactions to it. If we make these shifts quickly enough, we spur things along at a rapid pace, and the action and suspense benefit. Note, too, the conflict here: The two characters are not viewing the same event (the opening of the door) in the same manner—he wants to walk away, she's ambivalent, and this means they are close to a confrontation.

Which, as we know, is one of the pillars of conflict.

Quick point-of-view shifts are useful conflict-setters, too, because they can depict the tension in only a few lines. One sentence even, perhaps only a few words. Go back and forth a couple of times, and the conflict is fully laden. Each time we shift the point of view we bring in a new perception, and there's no reason why that new perception can't be used to create conflict with the perception in the prior scene or chapter.

All of this makes for more complete action and suspense, of course, because both rely so much on the development of conflict. Think of the possibilities for quick point-of-view shifts:

- two or more characters viewing the same event or conversation but with different reactions

- two or more characters struggling with different but interconnected events or circumstances happening simultaneously
- one character shifting between present and past, two different events but possibly the same reaction

Much is possible with shifting points of view, so long as we make the shifts quick and decisive. Once we've decided to develop the story this way — to set the stage — the action and suspense to follow will certainly be spurred.

A caveat, however: Quick point of view shifts work best when they aren't overdone. Too many will turn the drama down and make the reader yawn. Three or four in a row push the limit, and then we should back off . . . until it's time to rekindle the fire.

It is, after all, the reader we wish to intrigue, and the more opportunities there are to spark the reader's attention, the more success we'll have in making that intrigue last from cover to cover.

DIG THAT CONTRAST!

Most readers have expectations about characters, story settings, and story tone and mood. They *expect* one attractive character to be paired with another; they *expect* ominous events to emanate from ominous physical settings (or happy circumstances to result from pleasurable surroundings); they *expect* criminals to be disagreeable, priests to be saintly, professors to be intellectual, athletes to be insensitive, therapists to be approachable. . . .

They *expect* the world to spin logically, systematically. And why not? It's what most of us have been taught to believe. There is order to our world, a system of rules and inevitable results. For example,

- you commit a crime, you pay a penalty.
- you take more than your share, someone will suffer.
- you seek confrontation, you will find it.

We use expectations to structure our lives and to keep every-thing orderly and predictable. Good for getting us through the days.

But *not* so good for writing a lively story.

Expectations are like clichés; we rely on them because we know they usually work in real life, but that doesn't mean they belong in a piece of prose. They leave no surprise, no uncer-tainty, and in fiction, if we squeeze out the surprises, we have little to enjoy.

So, as writers, we know to avoid clichés, and we should also know to discombobulate readers' expectations. We have to gen-erate something unexpected, something unusual! We have to make the reader admit, *now here's something out of the ordinary.*

We have to look for contrasts, differences that skewer expec-tations and build dramatic impact.

Take characterizations. An attractive woman, an attractive man. Simple equation . . . and totally expected. What if one of them was grossly disfigured, and they still paired up? Or one of them outweighed the other by two hundred pounds, and they still paired up? Or one of them was mute and the other was blind, and they still paired up?

Whatever the reader's usual expectations, we offer some-thing different, and the most effective way is to develop con-trasts. Tall-short, young-old, dark-light, silent-talkative, cul-tured-boorish, selfish-generous.

Contrasting the characters develops the sense of conflict in the story, which, in turn, will spur the action and the suspense. But we *start* with the contrast, and that sets the stage for what's to follow.

How about *Beauty and the Beast*? Or Lady Chatterley and Mellors, the gamekeeper? Or Gatsby and Dolly? What of Heath-cliff and Catherine; Dart and Leila, in Erica Jong's *Any Woman's Blues* (Harper & Row); Lolita and Humbert? There are major contrasts between each pair of characters, some because of looks, others because of age, still others because of economic station. The deeper we make that contrast, the more interesting the relationship becomes because readers — more than anything a prisoner of their expectations—have to wonder how in the world it works.

And that gets us off and running with the story.

Contrast, though, comes in more than characterizations. We can use it to set the stage with description and setting, too. Here again expectations play a role. A burned-out urban lot with crumbling buildings and strewn garbage, for instance, would have us thinking that nothing of beauty could ever be found there. Yet, perhaps there's a tiny rose garden in a corner, or a homeless person living there who radiates a certain inner charm, or lying beneath the surface there's a breathtaking archaeological find.

Contrasts. Think how each of the physical settings could develop into a tension-filled event, which could then spill over into action and suspense. Suppose vandals deliberately stomped the rose garden, and the gardeners treated it as a personal attack upon their one vestige of beauty in a harsh, unforgiving world. Couldn't this escalate into danger and violence? Wouldn't we have action and suspense in the making?

Contrasts like these can happen in something as small as a single room (beautifully furnished with Sheraton sideboard, Currier and Ives prints, Steuben glass figurines . . . and a Ping-Pong table smack in the middle of the floor), or as large as an entire estate (a beautiful home with a weed-choked lawn, dying hedgerows and wilted flowers). Just as with characterizations, contrast in physical settings will catch readers' attention because it is not what they expect. And the nature of the unexpected is to raise the level of conflict, which, in turn, brings inevitable action and suspense. In Theodore Dreiser's *An American Tragedy*, Clyde, an ambitious, educated young man, has impregnated Roberta, a local factory worker. But Clyde has higher sights, and he has become friendly with a wealthy young crowd (who know nothing of his relationship with Roberta). One day Clyde and his friends are on a motor trip to a nearby lake when they come upon a weather-beaten farmhouse. Clyde jumps out to ask directions and he spots Roberta's father's name on the mailbox. He surveys the house:

So lonely and bare, even in this bright, spring weather! The decayed and sagging roof. The broken chimney to the north—rough lumps of cemented field stones lying at its base; the sagging and semi-toppling chimney to the south, sustained in place by a log chain. The unkempt path from the road below. . . .

Here stands Clyde, dressed fashionably, the expensive car idling behind him, facing bare-bones poverty. The contrast between the dilapidated farmhouse and the spiffy young people couldn't be more vivid. The suspense comes when Clyde has to ask directions, even though he is sure Roberta has shown his photo to her father.

And so the story moves forward.

Contrasts in physical setting can occur anywhere there is physical dimension—on a ship (a beautiful yacht where murder and torture take place, for example), an island (a botanical research station where diabolical human experiments occur), a slaughterhouse (where two adorable kittens cavort and play to the delight of the workers and public). The point is to think in terms of contrast, especially when you are in the early stages of putting your story together. It will develop conflict almost automatically—really.

And then if you want to add further contrast, think in terms of the overall tone of your story. Is it to be horror, or mystery, or suspense, or straight action? Will it seek to unseat the reader's assumptions or will it merely confirm them? With contrast, we skewer the reader's expectations, and when it comes to the story's tone, we do it by twisting things a bit. For example, why couldn't a mystery story be told through the eyes of a seven-year-old, or a horror story told (as Anne Rice does) by a vampire? Why couldn't a suspense story be set two thousand years in the future, or an action story be told through back-and-forth faxes?

The tone of a story is its class or kind—mystery, suspense, horror, etc.—and here we can dabble with contrast. George Higgins often uses humor zingers to spice the descriptions and the dialogue of the lowlifes he characterizes; and Donald Westlake writes humorous suspense through the blurry telescope of burglar John Dortmunder, who is one of the most inept criminals in current literature. Both of these writers take a story dealing with crimes and criminals—serious and deadly business—and make us laugh and laugh.

They contrast the *tone* of their stories with their story lines, and they don't lose one ounce of conflict.

And they set the stage for the story itself.

CHAPTER 3

OPENINGS

WILLIAM ZINSSER HAS written that readers are fickle souls, switching allegiances and attentions with unsettling speed. From the first word, they want to know "what's in it for them," how do they become a part of things, what can they expect to feel?

Woe to the writer who doesn't deliver.

With fiction and the great majority of nonfiction, the opening is the most important segment of the work, not because it may contain extraordinary literary deployment (though that could be the case, of course), but because if we lose on readers here, we'll never get them back. In tennis we get a second serve; in most types of writing we don't. We get only one chance to intrigue our readers, and we'd better make it work!

Stories rely on a developing conflict to generate interest and a sense of identification. If the opening is squishy or dull, it doesn't matter how exciting or eye-grabbing the remainder of the book is, the reader will have already put it aside. We have to start at a point where something is happening, *and we have to make it interesting*.

Interesting. Attention-getting. Dramatic.

Most experienced writers agree: If the reader isn't intrigued by the third page (some even say by the second page), we've lost the game. Part of the reason concerns expectations — the reader's, not the writer's. Dust jackets that proclaim "Cover to Cover Suspense!" "Riveting Action!" "A Thriller All the Way!" and advertisements that trumpet these blandishments give the reader a sense of what's to come. And if the first few pages

35

don't measure up, there's a quick letdown, and a search for something else.

Part of the reason, also, is that readers read to be entertained. They may read for other purposes, as well, but they want to be entertained, and our job is to see that entertainment happens. Any writer who forgets this will suffer the fate of the comedian who decided to get serious with his audience . . . and found himself playing to an empty hall.

By the end of page two, we should be entertaining the reader, we should be developing the strands of the story and building conflict. It doesn't have to be much, but the reader has to sense what's to come and be wondering what's going to happen next. Remember, we're building a story, not publishing literary philosophy or mannered symbolism. The reader expects something more than general discourse on esoteric or metaphysical themes, and that expectation quivers with anticipation. Fail to satisfy the anticipation — quickly — and it will fade away, leaving a blob of disinterest.

Take a look at some of the highly praised action and suspense novels of recent years: John Le Carre's *The Spy Who Came in From the Cold* (Franlin Watts), Scott Turow's *Presumed Innocent* (Farrar, Straus, Giroux), Mario Puzo's *The Godfather* (Putnam). In each one, by page three, some form of conflict has been established, and the roiling undertone of suspense has begun to develop. The reader's interest is piqued, and the story has started to build.

You can't do this if you start too far away from the hub of the story. What happens is that you find yourself scrambling to catch up. I recall a television documentary on skiing I was scripting, and a well-meaning actor suggested we open with a long shot from a plane circling the ski area, showing the snowy mountain peaks and valleys, offering a panorama of a beautiful winter scene. We'd circle for a while, and then he suggested we'd slowly zoom in on the skiers. The director and I listened politely, but both of us grew impatient. Before I could speak, the director said, "What is this, Film 101?"

The actor was puzzled. "Skiing's the theme, okay?"

"Action's the theme," the director said. "People *doing* things, in this case skiing." He turned to me. "How would you open?"

"Gauzy close-up of a skier," I said. "Quick body movement, grunting, spraying snow."

The director nodded. "Action sets the tone. See?"

Keep those openings inside the story's hub; it prevents dreamy posturing and far-out story connections. Remember, we don't want to sneak up on the story. Bring the reader in from the beginning, and you'll be surprised how effective the opening can be.

LEADS AND HOOKS

Yes, there are ways to collar the reader from the first line of the story. Yes, there are ways to hold the reader in thrall until the interest and sense of identification take over along about page three.

Leads and hooks, we call them. Consider:

> Freddie shuddered as Vito's sun-tanned face slowly hardened. Sweat beads made icy trails from his underarms in spite of the broiling sun. "I-I th-thought I had 'til tomorrow," he stammered. A whisp of ocean breeze brought more cold sweat. "It's tomorrow, right?"
> "Depends," Vito grunted.

This is from a suspense-mystery I published a few years ago. Note how the opening lines set the conflict and menace. The confrontation between the two characters begins by the second word ("shuddered") and then builds. This is the *shocker* type of lead because it explodes into the reader's consciousness. There's not much subtlety at this point, only quick dramatic impact, but that's what we mean to do.

We hook the reader by using action verbs (as we saw in chapter two) and developing an immediate conflict. The reader's attention is what we seek, and the reader's attention is what we'll get.

The shocker lead isn't the only choice, of course. What we're trying to do is get the reader interested, and we can do that by more subtle means. For example, we can portray a setting that offers no racehorse (highly charged, fast-paced, action-oriented) prose, but can suggest conflict and confrontation:

> On a July noon in 1978, Judge Joginder Nath entered his modest courtroom in Old Delhi to make known his long-awaited decision. His chamber was thronged, in a state of agitation, each person present having passed through a gauntlet of soldiers with fixed bayonets.

These are the opening lines of *Serpentine* (Doubleday), Thomas Thompson's re-creation of the diabolical crimes of Charles Sobhraj during the mid-1970s. Note how measured these words are, not at all frantic like the lead in the prior example. Yet we get a sense of immediate suspense because of where the action takes place—a courtroom. An agent said to me once, "Trials always sell well," and what she meant was that the nature of a trial includes built-in conflict and readers are hooked right away. In *Serpentine*, this is what we have, and the courtroom setting develops it. The key is to open with an intriguing setting, such as a courtroom (or a police interrogation room or a hospital operating room) and allow the built-in conflict to draw the reader in.

Leads and hooks can take other forms. The thing to remember is to build that conflict so the action and suspense can proceed. We can open with violence:

> Angie twisted the pinky ring so he could squeeze the steel-ball ornament in his closed palm. When he clobbered the bagman in the next few seconds, he didn't want him getting up.

Or we can open with *mystery*:

> Angie patted himself down again. He'd put the wallet in his back pocket, he remembered doing it . . . but it was

gone! The girl's address, without it he'd never pick up the drawer key.

Or we can open with *danger*:

> Angie held his breath. The large fin was circling closer, and there was no way he could outswim it. The electric prod in his hand was a matchstick compared to the huge fish's body.

What's common in all three of these openings is the quick conflict that entices the reader. Within a line or two some particular problem has been portrayed, and now the reader wants to see how it's resolved. Remember, our readers want to be entertained, and this gives the writer a head start. We don't have to develop our credibility *first* before our readers will allow themselves to be entertained. We have an audience already primed by the fact that they have picked up our book or story and are seeking to be entertained. We are credible right off the bat.

But if we don't push the entertainment along, that credibility will fade in a moment. It is not something we should take for granted.

On the other hand, what's entertaining can be widely varied. We can have leads and hooks that spring from *erotica*:

> It was the most beautiful morning of lovemaking I ever experienced ... her hands were soft cushions of velvet against my straining urgency.

Or from *bizarre circumstances*:

> It was a cemetery ... and it wasn't. No stones or markers, yet rounded earth humps spread across the field in some predetermined design.

Or from *anger*:

> Two dime-sized red spots appeared on his cheeks, and his words were suddenly cold. "You were the one," he said,

"not your brother, only you." He began to pound his fist into his open hand.

Think conflict with leads and hooks. Remember, we're trying to grab the reader early and keep the entertainment bells ringing page after page.

A BLOCK TO BUILD UPON

It may seem obvious, but it bears emphasizing: The opening of any story must form the foundation for what is to follow. It must be a block—sturdy and uncompromising—to build the rest of the story upon. If the opening is weak or fuzzy or of little relevance to the rest of the book, two unfortunate things will happen:

- The reader will become confused.
- The writer will be resented.

And that's assuming the reader hasn't closed the book after page two and gone on to something else. That wouldn't be unfortunate, it would be a calamity. But let's rely on our readers' loyalty for a moment. They hang with us through page fifty, and now we're into the bowels of the story.

But there's that ineffective opening. Somehow, it sticks in the reader's mind; it always does, you know. These are the first words and thoughts the reader faces, and the reader tends to remember them, even at page fifty. *Why did the writer begin like that? Is the beginning a part of the story? I'm confused!*

If there isn't a good linkage, the reader turns on the writer. *The writer's playing games and isn't well organized. Why should I keep reading this stuff?*

Slam! goes the book. One reader lost.

The opening must start things off well because there will be a progression of conflict-laden events that will lead to a conclusion somewhere down the line (remember "Escalate, Escalate!" in chapter one?) If that opening doesn't push the reader to the next event in some kind of orderly way, the story itself runs the risk of breaking down. That opening has to set the tone for everything that follows, and it better be sturdy enough. For example, if we were dealing with a mystery at sea, we wouldn't want to begin with a rambling discourse about the romance of the sea and the artful meshing of clouds and birds and weather and water in a paean to nature. This isn't, after all, an updated *Moby Dick*. It's a sea story with an emphasis on action and suspense. (Although, let's be clear about one thing: There *is* action and suspense in Melville's classic, but there's so much more, too.) So we would need an opening that forms a building block under the subsequent story. The block must contain:

- an event that will prove pivotal later.
- one or more characters who will figure prominently later on.
- a writing style that will set the tone for all that follows.

Consider this last: Would an opening that develops gradual psychological tension be a proper building block under a story that races from event to event? Probably not. The reader would only get confused because of the change in tone. Would a short, snappy opening be a better block? Probably.

Remember, though, the block must be sturdy enough, substantial enough to support the story to come. No one does this any better than the late John MacDonald in his Travis McGee novels. From page one we are enmeshed in the story that follows; the openings are truly sturdy blocks. Here's the way he begins *Free Fall in Crimson* (Harper & Row): a murder mystery about the death of a wealthy businessman, Ellis Esterland, and the fact that his only son, Ron, has inherited nothing. The story takes McGee into rural Florida, Beverly Hills, California and then Iowa as he attempts to piece the puzzle together:

> We talked past midnight, sat in the deck chairs on the sun deck of the *Busted Flush* with the starry April sky overhead, talked quietly, and listened to the night. Creak and sigh of hulls, slap of small waves against pilings, muted mo-

tor noises of the fans and generators and pumps aboard the work boats and the play toys.

"I don't really know how the law works," Ron Esterland said. "But I would think that if you arranged someone's death, even if he were dying already, you shouldn't inherit. . . ."

From this beginning, the entire story begins to unfold. Note the conflict in Ron's dialogue and the mention of inheritance and possible murder. Note, too, the touch of atmosphere in the first paragraph. McGee lives on a houseboat (don't you wish you did?) in tropical, lush Florida (gentle breezes, soft nights, brilliant sky), and we come to find out he works for himself. The ultimate rugged individualist, a professional in a trade where you can get killed. Now, we know all this by page three, and anyone who isn't caught up in the story doesn't deserve to be. John MacDonald has created his building block well because everything that occurs in the opening pages will be linked to something that occurs later on. Even in the few lines quoted—murder, inheritance, Florida nights—everything tied in.

That's the way we set our opening. As a block to build the story on. The action and suspense will flow. Guaranteed.

SOMETIMES DIALOGUE, SOMETIMES NARRATIVE

Most of us grow up writing narrative before dipping our toe into dialogue waters, and the reason is quite apparent. People *told* us stories before we learned how to write, and most storytellers tend toward narration (with an occasional dramatic exclamation that pass for dialogue). We listened, and naturally, when we started to write, we offered narrative, too.

Dialogue came later, as we learned to read and realized we could "hear" words on the page. Now, of course, we use dialogue and narrative interchangeably, but that doesn't mean either isn't more appropriate in some circumstances. For example, if we want to open by presenting an emotional reaction such as fear, we could do it through narration:

He was afraid. He didn't realize it until he noticed his shaking hands. Then the message went to his brain. *I'm afraid of my best friend, and all he's offering is a cigarette.*

Or we could do it through dialogue:

"You got the shakes, man," Jimmy said, offering him a cigarette.

"You almost killed her," he said, "you scare me, sometimes."

"Yeah," Jimmy grinned, showing his brown teeth, "your problem, you know?"

Which of the two openings is the more vivid? There's conflict in both, and there's budding suspense, too. But note which encourages the mental imagery, which tries to personify the fear.

The dialogue passage. We "hear" the words, and when they're conveyed with a not-so-subtle menace, they carry greater impact. That doesn't mean the narration wouldn't work, only that a dialogue opening might be more dramatic, especially when we're trying to portray a certain emotion. Fear, greed, horror, anger and jealousy are the kind of emotions that good dialogue conveys most effectively, because our senses are activated in an acute way. How does jealousy make us feel? Do we sense it through taste or smell or touch or sight?

"Her inheriting Mother's estate makes me want to chew wood chips."

or

"Whenever I see you touching one another, my headaches begin."

The images portray the emotion right before the reader, and by virtue of "hearing" the words, the reader gains greater involvement. It takes narration longer to accomplish this, and when we're opening our story, we don't have much time to get it done. So, with emotions we're better off opening with dialogue.

But narrative openings certainly have their place. The first thing to remember when using them, however, is to get that conflict in there. Keep in mind that as we describe and narrate we should inject an element or two of tension. Drama is the reason, and grabbing the reader's attention is the result. Here's the way Tony Hillerman begins *Coyote Waits* (Harper & Row), his suspenseful tale of murder and anthropology on the Navaho Reservation:

> Officer Jim Chee was thinking that either his right tire was a little low or there was something wrong with the shock on that side. On the other hand, maybe the road grader operator hadn't been watching the adjustment on his blade and he'd tilted the road.

The narration goes on for half a page, and then the author injects some dialogue, which lasts for another half page, before resuming the narration. But note the conflict in the opening: The first sentence indicates a problem, and the second sentence adds an additional element of uncertainty. It's man against his environment, a classic conflict builder. And when the dialogue does come in, the tension is heightened because now we "hear" the character's vexation with his vehicle and the surroundings.

The difficulty with a narrative opening is that it loses steam after a while (unlike dialogue, which can continue to unfold just like a stage play). There's a limit to effective narration as an opening because tension has a fairly short life, and we can't whip the narration along when the tension has petered out. For this reason and because the reader expects stories with action and suspense to develop smartly, we'd better be prepared to move into some dialogue by page three.

That old page three, where we lose the readers' interest *at the latest*, if we haven't hooked them. It's the same equation for narrative openings. Dialogue offers a change in pace (which all stories need) and a rejuvenation of conflict, but the unbroken narrative better not go beyond page three.

Yet narrative works well when we're building suspense, better, in fact, than dialogue, which has an immediacy that can bring things to a head quickly. With narration we can begin quietly and work up to something more substantial, taking a few pages to do it. Dialogue, on the other hand, would demand a speedier resolution.

Narration also works well if we open with an action sequence. The description of a car race, for example, or a bullfight, or a burglary, or a sea rescue could move up to that wall at page three without a line of dialogue, and the reader would continue to be enthralled because . . . the end is still in doubt. The race winner hasn't been declared, the bull continues to charge, the jewels haven't been found, the boat continues to founder. We can paint these scenes with narrative, and the reader is with us step-by-step.

And that's what counts, of course. Dialogue openings have their place, as do narrative openings. The more immediate we wish to be, we use dialogue; the more studied we wish to be, we use narration.

But never forget that too much of a good thing doesn't work. Change of pace, the wall at page three, the type of story we're developing, these are the keys.

So, open well . . . and don't forget your conflicts.

WHEN THE ENDING COMES FIRST

Most books and stories have a chronological life. They start at a certain point and move forward to some later end. Time is a crucial and controlling event because time determines story pace and story development. We are used to thinking of time in linear fashion, as a yardstick that measures story progress, and as time moves along the yardstick so does story development. "Begin at the beginning!" legions of writing instructors have demanded, and for most of their students that means starting the action at one point in time and moving the action *and* the time forward in lockstep. It's logical (because our reality is based on time "moving on"), it's orderly, and it's commonly followed.

But savvy writers know that merely because something is

generally done, doesn't mean it must *always* be done. In fact, the more innovative we can be, the more opportunity there is for fresh and lively prose. Anything that's "different" for the reader will gain that reader's attention, and if our approach is well thought out and smoothly presented, we will probably make more of an impact. (A caveat: Being different for the sake of being different doesn't cut it; there has to be *purpose* in our innovation, and it can't confuse the reader; the story must still flow well and proceed in some logical sequence.)

Chronological time, however, is not the rigid master we tend to think it is, and as writers we can twist it a bit, maneuver it and even invert it. Time—linear time, that is—becomes a writing technique we can play with, and by doing this we add something unusual to our story and just possibly rivet the reader's attention.

In particular, we can take time and stand it on its head; we can take the ending of a story and put it in the beginning, that is, we can open by showing the story's ending.

Why would we do this? Generally, of course, there's the idea of being innovative, of gaining the reader's attention in a different manner. More specifically, however, putting the ending out front allows us to work the story against it, to show how all the story lines progressed to that final point. Some readers, and writers, find enjoyment in the process of story development (the how and the why, not the what). Knowing the ending, for them, merely acts as a wall against which the story continues to resonate and rebound. The individual steps taken to reach the ending are what fascinate.

A classic example of how well this works is in Gabriel Garcia Marquez's *Chronicle of a Death Foretold* (Knopf) where the opening lines tell how the story will end:

On the day they were going to kill him, Santiago Nasar got up at five-thirty in the morning to wait for the boat the bishop was coming on. He'd dreamed he was going through a grove of timber trees where a gentle drizzle was falling.

Even the title of this novel announces how it will end: a story of *a death foretold* . . . a death that has already been described. And in the first line of the book we see that Santiago Nasar will be killed at some point during the day. The author gives away his plot in the first few words, and for those of us who appreciate suspense, this hardly seems to make sense. After all, the one undeniable fact in suspense is that it *keeps us guessing*. We don't know, for sure, what's going to happen.

So here comes this Nobel Prize winner, and he gives away the ending right off the bat! Santiago Nasar remains a central character throughout, but how do we retain our interest in his story, if we know he's going to be killed? Where's the suspense?

What we don't know is whether the killing will be successful, who wants to kill him and why, and that's the key to this book. And because Gabriel Garcia Marquez paints his characters so vividly and develops his scenes with emotionally riveting cross-currents, we remain fascinated. Conflict jumps out at the reader page after page, and in spite of knowing the ending, suspense continues to build.

Note that after the quoted opening above, the author mentions that Santiago's mother is adept at interpreting his dreams (we're still early on page two):

> . . . but she hadn't noticed any ominous augury in those two dreams of her son's, or in the other dreams of trees he'd described to her on the mornings preceding his death.

Then, six lines later (still on page two):

> Furthermore: all the many people he ran into after leaving his house at five minutes past six and until he was carved up like a pig an hour later remembered him as being a little sleepy but in a good mood.

Now, we even know how he died and when. But the actual description of his death doesn't come until the final pages. Everything else merely leads up to it, and that's why this works so well: *We want to understand because the author has engaged our sympathy.*

Why, we ask, why? And we continue reading.

Some writers, perhaps mindful that readers could object to knowing how a story ends before they finish page one, disguise their efforts—but not their effect—by giving away the ending in an introduction or prologue. It's not the actual story, they seem to be saying, it's a teaser or a backgrounder, don't take it too seriously, don't jump into the plot with it.

The benefit is that this still sets up that wall to work against, in spite of the cavalier spin the author may wish to put on the significance of the opening section. We *do* know the ending, and that means the action and suspense must work against it. The disadvantage is that the reader might get turned off knowing the ending so early, but if we develop our story well, creating memorable characters and circumstances, the reader should remain interested in *why* things happened.

Take a look at Russell Banks's *Continental Drift* (Harper & Row), the story of the clash between two cultures, Haitian and American. Banks calls his opening pages "Invocation" (not "Introduction," and certainly not "Chapter One"), and he begins:

> It's not memory you need for telling this story, the sad story of Robert Raymond Dubois, the story that ends along the back streets of Miami, Florida, on a February morning in 1981 . . . the story that tells what happened to young Bob Dubois in the months between the wintry afternoon in New Hampshire and the dark wet morning in Florida.

Before the opening sentence is finished we know who and when and what and where . . . all we don't have is why. Russell Banks has given us the ending, and if we interpret just a bit, we can figure out that the "sad story" concerns the death of Bob Dubois on that back street in Miami sometime after the story begins. Yet, does this detract from our reading of the story and our interest in it? Here again, it's the development of character and the solid story line (including drugs, murder, voodoo, sex and smuggling) that keep our interest. Conflict abounds, and before we know it, we're caught up in *why* Bob Dubois left New Hampshire, made it to Florida, and ended up transporting illegal aliens.

For the readers, the allure is clear. From page one we know the ending.

And that's a lot more than any of the characters know.

CHAPTER 4

LEAVE 'EM HANGING

THE TRADITION OF *to be continued* is part of our literary heritage, and it occupies a firm place in any tale where action and suspense flower. Think back to the stories of Charles Dickens in the nineteenth century and his newspaper serializations that appeared biweekly or monthly, each one taking the reader to an exciting precipice, only to stop and announce *to be continued*.

The next issue—breathlessly awaited—would pick up the story, and the process would be repeated. Dickens, himself, admitted he would stretch out his stories, deliberately fashioning them so they would reach that exciting precipice in each issue. He knew the value, he said, of placing his readers in suspense and walking away.

He would leave 'em hanging!

We see *to be continued* in forms beyond literature—soap operas on television, for example. Is there ever a day when the story on screen doesn't end with some moment of high drama, some unresolved conflict, some sudden accusation? The television producers leave the audience hanging, as the screen image dissolves and the music swells in an ominous crescendo. Wait! the program says, wait until tomorrow, we'll take care of this difficulty, this *conflict*, then.

In the meantime, hang there uncertain and wondering. You'll support us more avidly that way.

The fact that soap opera audiences number in the millions and have been supportive for generations says a lot about how successful this technique is. It works because audiences approach it with a double expectation:

- They expect to be left hanging.
- They expect to have the dilemma resolved.

It's the same thing with writing; readers have the identical expectations. We know that readers seek to be entertained, and we also know that they look to us to provide that entertainment.

So, one way to entertain them is to excite them, and one way to excite them is to leave them in the midst of a conflict.

That's drama, of course (because conflict *is* drama), and we know from chapter one how far that will take us when the story involves action and suspense. The point is that, when we leave readers hanging, we are really leaving them in the midst of a conflict in the story, and that's exciting and entertaining.

But readers expect this, especially with stories of action and suspense. So our job is to feed this expectation, and we do it by moving the story forward to an exciting point . . . and stopping. Think conflict, think dilemma, think surprise:

> . . . he watched the little Fiat's taillights blend with the Gross Platz traffic, and he turned away, knowing the plan was working. But, then, suddenly, there was a screech, the crash of crumpling metal, and the lights of Gross Platz seemed to jump like a thousand crazy eyes.

End of chapter, end of scene. Perhaps we don't get back to what happened for a number of pages, but don't worry, the readers won't forget. We've left 'em hanging by not showing what or who was in the crash and by not pursuing the story line further. The readers wonder, the readers are surprised, the readers may even guess what happens.

But the readers don't *know!*

And that's why they won't forget, and that's why they will stay interested and read on. Curiosity, something unresolved, it's human to pursue it.

Which brings us to the second of those expectations: Readers expect to have the dilemma or the conflict resolved. We can leave them hanging only for a limited time; otherwise, the conflict or the dilemma or the surprise ceases to have impact. Eventually, it recedes in importance as the story moves beyond it, and readers may then lose interest and faith in the writer. So, at some point we must release our readers by resolving the conflict or the dilemma or explaining the surprise. For example, take the action sequence above. A few pages later (no *more* than a few pages, either) we might start a new scene:

> He spied the smashed-up Fiat along the rear fence of the police-wrecker lot. Its twisted remains reminded him of a ghoulish, hideous mask, and he wondered if anyone else had noted it. Probably not, they'd scraped the metal carcass off the Gross Platz so fast, who had time for imagining?

Now we know what happened: The Fiat was in a major accident and, presumably, the driver was injured or killed. The readers aren't hanging any longer, and there are no unmet expectations.

Until the next build-up.

SCENE CUTS

One of the things that eludes some writers is the importance of procedural elements that beef up the content and the impact of the prose. It could seem a small matter because, arguably, no story should rise or fall on things such as untidy grammar, overly lengthy chapters or complicated construction. The content of the prose is what's supposed to count; the story line development, the characterizations, and the sense of place are supposed to offer substance and breadth.

The trouble is that most of the time these important parts don't work well unless they are presented in certain ways. They *do* depend on how they are presented. If not done right, story content, itself, suffers.

An example:

At last they had daylight between them and the gray boat. The finish line was but a hundred yards away, and if they could hold this tack, the cup would be theirs. "I think we're going to lose the race," Jennifer said to her grandfather on the committee boat, but the old man appeared not to have heard.

This is an action sequence, but note there are two separate scenes: one from the perspective of the competitors, one from the perspective of the spectators. Yet they are bunched into one paragraph, and thus the impact from either one is blunted. Think back to chapter two and the way we used scene cuts to dramatize a point-of-view shift. Each change became a separate scene, and here we have the same thing. Procedurally these two sequences need to be separated into individual scenes or separate paragraphs so the reader isn't confused by a quick change in point of view. Content-wise we need no changes: first the progress of the race, then the reactions of the spectators. But because the two sequences are run together, they bleed into one another and destroy the effectiveness of both.

A simple procedural device would make everything fine: Create separate scenes, end one with the growing certainty of how the race will end . . . then skip a couple of lines and begin the other with Jennifer's comment to her grandfather. We haven't changed any of the words or phrases, we haven't re-arranged the sentences; all we've done is separate them.

That's the way procedure beefs up content.

Scene cutting is another procedural device, and handled properly it can create conflict or it can add to existing conflict. It isn't a substantive technique because we aren't rewriting the prose or adding more story line—all we're doing is rearranging things or interrupting them.

Scene cutting means basically to move from scene to scene, or from point of view to point of view, quickly and dramatically. The movement, itself, is what enhances the conflict because it doesn't allow the reader to lie back and become immersed in the extended playing out of any scene. The scene ends . . . move!

Next scene . . . move!

Next scene . . . move!

And the reader grows more attentive and more excited as the level of tension rises.

In Dan Jenkins's novel, *You Gotta Play Hurt* (Simon & Schuster), the story of a year in the life of a cynical, wisecracking, successful magazine sportswriter, we see the character's disdain (and, therefore, the tension setup) for those who don't share his profession or his jaded view of life. One scene ends at a Winter Olympics cocktail party with the sportswriter running into a phoney Italian countess:

> She commented on what a handsome group we were—the magazine troops—and how exceedingly clever it was that we all worked for a living.

Next scene, which is the following day at breakfast. This is the opening:

> My hangovers tend to have a life of their own. My kind of hangover won't take yes for an answer, it feels like a hippopotamus slept on it.

This scene goes on for one page, there's some dialogue relating to meeting the magazine's new publisher (who likes to be called Clipper and is an adman caricature), then the sportswriter leaves the breakfast, and the scene ends:

> But I didn't leave without giving Clipper a hearty handshake and saying I thought he was going to bring a lot to the regatta.

Next scene, opening sentence:

> On the final night of the figure skating competition, the last event of the Winter Olympics, all of my friends were in the press section.

In the space of little more than a page, we've cut from a formal cocktail party to a hangover-laden breakfast to the final evening of competition in the ice stadium. We have *moved*!

And the quick cuts keep the reader's attention from straying. Is there conflict in here? We see the sportswriter's attitude toward the phoney Italian countess and the phoney adman publisher—he doesn't like them. The quick scene cuts point up an underlying conflict between the sportswriter and most of the nonwriters he deals with, and when it's portrayed against a background of international sports competition, there is action aplenty.

Note, however, that Dan Jenkins doesn't change point of view; everything is seen through the eyes of one character. The scene cuts, therefore, must have that character changing location quickly and often, in order to keep the tension high. If he stays in one place, quick scene cuts would be much more difficult.

But, now, let's also change points of view; let's add another character or two. Then, we don't have to worry so much about location. In fact, we can shift between different characters even though they are in the same room. But changing point of view allows us to develop *substantive* conflict (content, not process), as well as procedural conflict. Two or more characters can share opposite feelings, and by cutting back and forth between them we highlight that opposition. Or, if the characters are not in the same location, they don't have to be in opposition (though they can be, of course); the conflict heightens even if they are working toward the same goal. For example, an airport controller might be talking a damaged jumbo jet down to safety, and the story switches between the jet captain and the controller. These characters aren't in the same location, they aren't in opposition to one another, but their common goal is suspense-filled. If we cut back and forth quickly and often, we'll keep the level of conflict high, indeed.

Obviously, the benefits of quick scene cutting demand short scenes because procedural conflict will fade rapidly if we let it languish. One or two pages is the outer limit, but if the scenes can be reduced to half a page, or a single paragraph or even a single sentence, so much the better. We end each scene, no mat-

ter how short, with some unresolved dilemma (we leave 'em
hanging, remember), and we move to the next.
Quickly.

TRANSITIONS

As we slide from scene to scene, change is always implied. Characters change, places change, time changes whenever we pull
down the prose curtain and then hoist it again. Perhaps the
changes are minimal, but they are there, and it's the writer's job
to make them — and keep them — dramatic.

Time changes are crucial in any piece of prose because the
story will move forward, and the reader must be able to keep
up and to understand the changes. We call such changes "transitions," and they usually mean a new scene:

> . . . he walked into the filmy, purple dusk, and I wondered
> whether I'd ever see him again.

> One month later, I was coming out of the methadone
> clinic. . . .

And we add drama by ending one scene at a suspenseful moment and beginning the next at some point in the future. Time
has moved and so has the story and the drama. "One month
later" is the transition and it bridges the scenes.

In some ways transitions and scene cuts are alike: They are
devices for building procedural conflict, they precipitate changes
(in action, time, point of view, location), they prevent reader
bog-down (by not allowing things to remain static), and they can
move the story. But they are different, too: Transitions are part
of story content because they show the passage of time (*the next
day* . . . , *by early March* . . . , *six months after this* . . .) and the story
line must stay consistent with it. Scene cuts, on the other hand,
are procedural because they influence story content but are
never a part of the story. Also, transitions can develop *within* a
scene, but, of course, scene cuts must create separate scenes.

> . . . I gave him back the piece of blue glass, wondering what significance he saw in it. A couple of weeks later, I found out when he called me.

Note, however, that even though we don't have a separate scene, the sentence preceding the transition offers a dilemma or problem, something that will pique the reader's curiosity. Then the transition passage will attempt to resolve it.

Leave 'em hanging, of course.

Transitions also are useful devices for lengthening tension and apprehension. If we end a scene at a tense moment, then open the next scene hours or days later, the tension carries over (unless, of course, we dissipate it by resolving the issue right away):

> . . . "I can't talk to you any longer, I just can't," she cried, running off.

> Two hours later, she remained in her room, and my mind played back her words for the twentieth time.

Transitions can begin and end with either dialogue or narrative, but to build suspense, it's better to use them both, as the above passage shows. Dialogue offers the advantage of immediacy and quick drama (as we'll see later on in chapter five), and this is always useful. Narrative, however, allows a more thorough build-up, so it might be appropriate for purposes of picking up the story threads *after* the transition (as in the above example).

The key is this: Transitions should occur during tense moments; they should *not* resolve the problem or the dilemma or the confrontation, at least not right away. Allow the conflict to resonate for a while, and this will make the transition more significant and more useful.

Leave 'em hanging.

IT PAYS TO WAIT

One of the toughest writing skills to develop is a competent sense of pace, an ability to keep the story flowing smoothly even as mini-climaxes occur or events whipsaw or characterizations change. The tendency is to overemphasize at certain points and to underemphasize at others because of a failure to gauge the full track of the story from beginning to end. What it takes is an appreciation of the long view of the story and how each rise and fall in action, suspense, even tension, fits in. When, for example, should an action scene be introduced and how should it should play—understated, overdramatized, partially portrayed? If we limit ourselves to the parameters of the scene we're writing and ignore its role in the overall story, we can easily make the story lopsided and affect its sense of pace.

Story pace, essentially, means two things: smooth, even writing without anticlimaxes, without lengthy static prose; and carefully constructed scenes that blend with one another and build to a satisfying climax. Pacing our story means controlling it, and that, in turn, means taking the long view and measuring each scene against the entire story line. Would we want two action scenes back to back? Are the elements of suspense so unconnected as to destroy the threads of menace? We need to answer questions like these from the point of view of story pace because that's what'll determine how smoothly the story reads.

And how many readers we'll have at the end.

Load things in the beginning, and the reader's expectations are raised unnaturally high ("unnaturally" because most seasoned writers know that after a while what might have been exciting one hundred pages earlier, now becomes commonplace—which means *dull*—and the writer has nothing new to offer). Concentrate things in the middle, and what comes after is a sad anticlimax. Concentrate things at the end, and the change of pace might be so overwhelming as to seem contrived (the writer trying to "fix" the story in the last few pages).

So we pay attention to story pace (for more on all of this, see chapter eleven), and we remember to take the long view while still using an opening hook, as the last chapter showed. The point is to not rush the story. Instead, stretch it out so that doses of action and the suspense can be meaningfully employed. Here are some keys:

- Don't pick up the story threads too quickly.
- Let uncertainty fester in the reader.
- Stretch out rescues and solutions.
- Offer less than satisfactory alternatives to dilemmas and problems.

Wait . . . and then wait some more. This is especially important in stories where mood and atmosphere play a vital role. Don't give things away too quickly, a hint here, a hint there, a slow build-up, but nothing so determinative that readers figure out the ending long before the writer wants them to. Think of the suspense masters: Edgar Allan Poe, Shirley Jackson, Alfred Hitchcock. Things are *never* explained early, the menace and the uncertainty are allowed to fester and to grow. From time to time there will be a hint of what's to come, but nothing so specific that readers figure it all out . . . until the end.

In the meantime, we go back to the more sedate story line and work that for a while until it's time to get back into suspense or action. But even when we do come back, there's no reason to get it over quickly (an impressive example of how action can be stretched out is in Scott Spencer's *Endless Love* [Knopf] where one lovemaking scene covers more than thirty pages). We can begin with a seemingly innocent event—a man walking to the corner to get a pack of cigarettes, a girl selling Girl Scout cookies, a group of bird-watchers in the field—and the action can slowly develop as first one event and then another builds to confrontation.

Whatever happens, we want to stretch it out so the reader is unsure of the outcome for a while, and even when the scene ends, we don't want the reader completely satisfied. Have the man out for cigarettes rushed to a hospital in a coma from a gunman's bullet, have the Girl Scout cookie girl held prisoner in a darkened attic by an insane spinster, have the bird-watchers stalk a poacher who had just shot a bald eagle.

But wait for the next action scene to resolve these dilemmas! Leave 'em hanging right there—for the moment.

TO COMPLETE OR NOT TO COMPLETE

Most of us, at one time, have probably written something like the following:

> We settled comfortably on the sofa, and Alec took a final puff on his pipe before tapping its remnants into a coffee table ashtray. Outside, the snow continued to fall heavily, thickly, and we knew no one would be leaving before morning. Alec furrowed his brow and looked up. "Here's the way it was done," he said. "I've figured it out . . ."
>
> Suddenly, an eerie screech came from upstairs, followed by a crash and a thump.
>
> "My God!" Alec stared. "We've got to help. . . ." He jumped up and ran to the stairs.

Here's a little action and suspense, mixed together and served as drama. I say that most of us have written a scene like this (suspense, action overlapping) because it's such a common one—the cool sleuth, having sifted through the menaces in the house or on the island or within the family, has now deduced the solution. In a warm, beckoning setting (which makes everyone feel *good*) he is about to let us in on the explanation.

But then he's interrupted, and what had been warm and beckoning now becomes frightening and uncertain. There's been a shift of atmosphere, and our readers are jarred from complacency to apprehension. Just when they thought the solution would come, there's a hitch.

Our readers are left hanging.

For a moment, for a page or two, for a chapter or even for the entire book? Your decision, of course. After all, Alec doesn't have to be the one to come up with the solution. In fact, within the next few moments, Alec could no longer be alive.

So we're faced with two questions: Should we complete the business between the narrator and Alec where the solution is about to be offered? Should we, in effect, pick up the threads and resume?

Or, if we don't, how do we dispose of Alec and his budding solution?

The point is—at this moment—it doesn't matter (though eventually we'll have to decide). Instead, we should realize that by changing story pace in the middle of a scene, we have left our readers hanging.

We can leave our readers hanging *in the middle of a scene*, as well as at the end of a scene.

We can even do it in the middle of a paragraph:

> I hadn't seen those markings on the wall yesterday, the light was bad and I'd forgotten my glasses, but now . . . a shot rang out, somewhere behind. I looked for Caleb, but I only saw shadow.

Here, we leave our readers hanging by not explaining what the markings are, and instead we insert a bit of action to divert attention and spin the story off into another direction. Note that we begin with suspense (the uncertainty of the markings and their relevance to the story), and we quickly cut to action. We intertwine them for maximum effect, and if it's not done too often, it works well.

Obviously, with suspense material, we must place major emphasis on uncertainty and elusive solutions, all the while building the menace that challenges the characters. If we insert too much action, we shatter the delicate mood of anxiety we have tried to cultivate. Action is direct, forceful, while suspense is whispy, vague, even ephemeral. Keep them separate for the most part except when you want to leave the reader hanging.

How do we do it?

- Begin with something interesting, something dramatic to establish conflict.
- Stop! at a point where the reader doesn't expect it (the cusp of an explanation, the point of confrontation, the edge of victory or defeat).
- Satisfy yourself that the reader is intrigued, but don't give away the answer or explanation.

- Shift gears. If you've been doing suspense, change to action; if action, change to suspense.
- Follow the shift to its conclusion. (You don't want to leave 'em hanging too often—don't break *this* one off in the middle.)

Then decide whether you wish to go back and complete the explanation, confrontation or competition further along in the story. There's only one reason why you should see it through: *It must add to the story.*

If it doesn't, then forget about it. If it duplicates something else or is tangential or merely satisfies your peculiar sense of order (tying up loose ends, so to speak), it doesn't deserve any further attention. Go on with your tale and be content you've left 'em hanging.

Readers will love you for it.

CHAPTER 5

BUILDING THROUGH DIALOGUE

I HAD AN ASTUTE writing teacher in high school, and one day he asked us to reconstruct a recent disagreement we might have had with our parents. As it happened, my parents and I had argued the night before over my cavalier attitude about weekend curfews. I railed against any limitations, and they, of course, insisted there be some.

The incident seemed a neat fix for what the teacher had asked, so I reproduced what my parents and I had said to one another. What could be more realistic than that? I sat back and waited for the compliments.

Only they didn't come. Instead, the teacher took me aside and told me that what I had given him wasn't a story, at all. "You're acting like a stenographer," he said.

"But that's what we said to each other," I protested.

He shook his head and pointed to the word *Dialogue*, which he'd written on the board. "Learn to listen," he said, "don't try to memorize."

It took me a while to understand. And years later, I built on his advice.

"What's the difference between conversation and dialogue?" I now ask writing students.

"They're the same," someone always says.

"One's spoken, the other's written," another might add.

I shake my head. "Is this dialogue? 'Hello . . . how are you? . . . I'm fine. . . . Good. . . . Yeah. . . .'"

Shrugs and blank faces.

"Is it conversation?" I ask.

"It's pretty dull," a voice usually offers.

"Should dialogue be dull?"

They shake their heads. Then, from the back: "But conversation *can* be dull!"

"Conversation isn't dialogue," I respond. Conversation is the way we communicate with one another in daily living, and whether it's dull or not has little bearing. We converse to get a message out. But dialogue . . . ah, that's different. Dialogue is a medium of performance; it's what we use when we're writing a story. Dialogue is a special kind of conversation; it's conversation with drama!

So, the throwaway words of conversation such as "Hello," "How are you," "I'm fine," "Good" should never be thought of as dialogue . . . *because they don't contain drama*. Don't reproduce conversation and call it dialogue; reproduce only that portion of the conversation that has the drama:

Not: Hello, how are you?

But: I've got to talk with you. Something important. . . .

Listen to the words, don't memorize them.

The key to good dialogue is to remember Anthony Trollope's advice of more than a century ago: Dialogue must contribute to telling the story. If it doesn't, it's of no use. So, words of conversation that have no dramatic impact won't do much for our story, and they had better be removed. They aren't dialogue, as we've just seen. But when mystery-suspense writer Tony Hillerman has his Navaho tribal policemen, Lieutenant Joe Leaphorn and Sergeant Jim Chee, discuss finding an ivory-colored bead as part of a murder investigation in *Skinwalkers* (Harper & Row), we see a classic case of dialogue moving the story along:

"Where was it?"

"On the floor under the bunk. Maybe it fell out when I changed the bedding."

"What do you think?" Leaphorn asked.

"I think I never had anything that had beads like that

on it or knew anybody who did. And I wonder how it got here."

"Or why?" Leaphorn asked.

In a few short lines we've come a distance, and it's all because of the dialogue, which has certainly provided dramatic impact. The bead has raised an ominous question or two and has become an important part of the unfolding story. Anthony Trollope would nod sagely.

But Trollope, with all due respect, had a limited vision about dialogue. There is another purpose dialogue can serve, one that could be used in place of the requirement to move the story along. Dialogue can also be used to develop character, to show us the side or sides of one or more characters. Note I write *show*, not tell, because it's important to understand that the character must be *portrayed* by the dialogue, not simply described by it. Here again we're dealing with drama, and when we show a character through dialogue, we do it dramatically:

"You will not succeed," he said, his voice like ice. "I will not have it."

Dialogue becomes a tool for building the reader's apprehensions and interest. Before we can develop the story, however, we must understand that when dialogue disintegrates into dull conversation, it destroys the forward movement of the tale, and once this happens, the conflict falls apart and the action and suspense hold no one's interest. Keep your dialogue within the twin parameters of moving the story forward (as Anthony Trollope insisted) and developing characterization. This will go a long way toward spurring drama and sparking the reader's urge to turn the pages.

YES/NO

We know from chapter one that the most obvious form of conflict is confrontation, and that confrontation develops scenes of action and suspense. Readers are interested in confrontation because the drama inherent in a face-off carries excitement and uncertainty. Who will prevail, how *do* they prevail, where does this leave other characters and circumstances? Questions like these flash through readers' minds even as the moment of confrontation is played out and the story, itself, proceeds.

Dialogue, of course, is an excellent tool for developing confrontation. There is no clearer way to portray disagreement or opposition than by having two or more people face one another down by means of dialogue. "Yes/No" is what I call dialogue that carries direct confrontation:

> "I'm calling the police!"
> "You'd better wait."
> "We must tell them."
> "Not tonight, we don't."

There's no equivocation here, there's only direct disagreement. It will work well for a short time, providing we keep the excitement building; that is, we don't allow the disagreement to remain at a static level: "yes, no, yes, no, yes, no. . . ." There must be a change of pace or the introduction of something new, such as a third voice or intrusion by an external event. Watch the way Jack London did it in his well-known boxing story "The Mexican," in which a scrawny young man walks into a promoter's office and volunteers to go into the ring with a world-class fighter. The fight promoter eyes him with disdain, and the young man responds impassively:

> "I can lick Ward," was all he said.
> "How do you know? Ever see him fight?"
> Rivera shook his head.
> "Haven't you anything to say?" the fight promoter snarled.
> "I can lick him."
> "Who'd you ever fight, anyway?" Michael Kelly demanded. Michael was the promoter's brother. . . .

Here's a short Yes/No sequence, followed by a further build-up.

The fighter and the promoter disagree about the fighter's skills (Yes/No), and then because Jack London didn't want the disagreement to grow static, he introduced a third character, the promoter's brother, who continued the confrontation but in a less direct manner (and built up the tension by broadening it). This is clearly an action story, and Jack London does describe the fight in great detail. But this early confrontation between the fighter and the promoter establishes two things: The essential conflict and the immediacy of the action—both amply set forth by the dialogue and the drama that accompany the confrontation. It wouldn't have been so dramatic if Jack London had used narrative to describe the fighter's self-assurance and the promoter's suspicion:

> The young man looked the promoter in the eye and told him he could lick Ward. The promoter didn't believe him and challenged him to say if he'd ever seen Ward fight. Michael Kelly, the promoter's brother, then demanded to know who he'd ever fought.

Which version has the drama, which version conveys impact and immediacy? The dialogue, of course, and when the promoter's brother steps in, the confrontation builds because new elements have been injected—a third person and a new line of questioning. So Jack London avoids putting his Yes/No dialogue confrontation into a static hold; he keeps it moving by building it to a new level.

And that's one way the action and the suspense grow.

WELL/MAYBE

Something I stress with inexperienced writers is that humans are rarely *directly* responsive to one another, especially when conversing. More often, responses will be oblique or partial:

> "Would you tell me your name, please?"
> "Why're you asking?"

Often, our minds are on what we'll say when the other person finishes, and we don't listen carefully to the words coming at us. We'll usually pick up the mood and perhaps the gist, but we want to get our own words in. For example:

"The cold bites tonight."

And if we're listening carefully, we might respond:

"It makes my fingers tingle."

But if we're concerned with getting home before midnight, we might say:

"I'll get locked out if we don't hurry."

The second choice is not responsive, but that doesn't make it any less interesting. In fact, it's probably more appropriate, given the modest listening skills of most people. As writers, we have to recognize that written dialogue must reflect this human trait. Instead of a direct response, quite often we should use an indirect response, or even an unresponse. In terms of confrontations and conflict, rather than use Yes/No dialogue, we might find it more appropriate to use "Well/Maybe"—an indirect, oblique response:

"I wish you'd watch where you're walking."
"God, these cobwebs are gross."

Indirect here, but we don't lose the sense of conflict, do we? Instead of the second character saying, "I *am* being careful!" or "I couldn't help it!" we create an obligue dialogue passage that is partially responsive (the cobwebs could cause ducking and stumbling) but also expands the scene (now we know there are eerie cobwebs).

This is Well/Maybe.

There are several ways to handle it:

- Answer a question with a question.
- Let two or three dialogue passages go by before answering an earlier question.
- Mimic the speaker's line.
- Interrupt the speaker.
- Don't answer what happened, but say why it happened.

Let's take this last:

> "I want to know where you were last night. The police have called three times!"
> "Did they find Harry's car? Did they find my boots?"

Note that the second speaker is not answering directly, not telling where he was the night before. Instead, he's offering a reason why he may have been somewhere that caused the police to get involved. He might have been searching for Harry's car and/or his boots, or . . . he might have been involved in something that caused the loss of Harry's car and/or his boots. We won't know the full answer unless we go through a few more dialogue passages, but here, at least, the response is indirect enough so the reader doesn't know the full answer.

And this will keep the suspense moving.

The Well/Maybe approach to dialogue has the advantage of avoiding story bog-down. By nature, indirect response injects something new in the interaction between speakers. No question completely answered, no thought fully portrayed, no agreement thoroughly made. There are equivocations and limitations in the dialogue responses with Well/Maybe, and this keeps the story moving because there is never enough to satisfy the reader's questions.

THREAT OF THE UNSAID

The experienced writer understands that dialogue cannot move at the same speed or intensity, that it must vary in the course of a chapter or even a single page. We understand the importance in building to a climax, and dialogue, which remains at a single speed, will have a tendency to undercut the climax. For example, imagine a story with racehorse dialogue, strong verbs, charged language:

> "You've got to cut off his wind!" Bob yelled, pointing at the blue-hulled *Avenger*. "Bring her hard right!"
> "The sails'll rip, they won't take the strain."
> "You want them to board us and find the stuff?" Bob's eyes were pinpoints of fire. He raised his fist to the sky. "No one's gonna take what we found!"
> "Hey! they're shooting at us. . . ."

This level of intense dialogue could go on for a little while, but imagine it stretching across several pages. Pretty soon the sense of apprehension and conflict would become commonplace because that's the only level the reader experiences. So the impact of the action slides until it carries little significance. The reader, after all, has been through this for pages, there's little surprise or menace that hasn't been absorbed.

The reader asks: What's for an encore?

The writer smiles weakly and shrugs. "Wish I knew."

One way to vary dialogue pace and at the same time build the story is to underplay, to do the opposite of throwing high-powered, dramatic-inspired words at the reader.

Be matter-of-fact in the midst of an emotional whirlwind; remain quiet while others shout; use few words when a major discussion erupts; show bare interest in a major discovery. All of these are forms of underplaying a scene, and they are particularly appropriate in stories of suspense where uncertainty is so important. Most readers expect consistent reaction to a sudden event, but what happens when at least one of the characters shows disinterest? When the unexpected reaction occurs, the reader is struck with uncertainty.

Take a look at the way short story writer Raymond Carver handled underplayed dialogue in his story "The Student's Wife." Mike and Nan, married and with two young children, have retired for the night, but Nan awakes before Mike can fall asleep, and she grows progressively manic, trying to prevent him from falling asleep before she does. She has just listed — aloud — all the things she likes:

> "You're asleep," she said.
> "I'm not," he said.
> "I can't think of anything else. You go now. Tell me what you like."
> "I don't know. Lots of things," he mumbled.
> "Well tell me. We're just talking, aren't we?"
> "I wish you'd leave me alone, Nan." He turned over to his side of the bed again and let his arm rest off the edge. She turned too and pressed against him.
> "Mike?"
> "Jesus," he said.

Nan's mania grows so severe that she stays up all night, stalking about the house, ending at dawn by falling to her knees and praying to God for help. There are deep-rooted problems in this marriage, yet Carver never describes them directly, preferring to highlight incompatibility in scenes such as the above. Note how he underplays: Nan is manic, Mike is barely conscious; Nan wants attention, Mike can't be bothered. Taken alone, Mike's reactions and dialogue are so minimal as to offer almost nothing. But when Nan's character is woven in, something sinister seems to intrude because we expect more from a husband, given his wife's growing agitation.

And that's how the threat of the unsaid works. By underplaying (being restrained, subdued) we are implying more than our words convey, and their impact, therefore, can be more devastating. Raymond Carver's story is suspenseful because we know that something isn't quite right, though we aren't able to pinpoint it, and we keep reading to try to uncover it. It's only at the end we see it is the marriage, itself, that needs attention, and then we sense the agony these two people are undergoing. The conflict's there, of course, and the threat of the unsaid allows the story to build because we're never sure where it's going to lead. Will they get along, will they agree, or will they break apart?

The threat of the unsaid—underplaying—tends to work better with suspense stories because it is a subtle technique, and action stories, or action scenes, tend to be pretty direct and unsubtle. It would be hard, for example, to fit in an underplayed give-and-go while characters are mountain climbing (it might work when they are settled for the night on a plateau or outcropping, but not while they are physically struggling), and it would be equally as difficult to underplay a sea rescue or a tennis match or a crime-in-progress, anything, in fact, where spirited action is developing.

But where the story has uncertainty, where anxiety rules while characters try to cope, the threat of the unsaid raises the level of menace because no one knows what to expect. The usual reactions to uncertainty and anxiety—frustration, impatience, fear—are heightened when a character underplays . . . and thus makes things that much more dramatic.

> "My God, don't you feel *anything*!"
> "I think I'm hungry."

SELF-TALK

There's more than one form of dialogue, as writing teachers are fond of pointing out; there's *exterior* dialogue, and there's *interior* monologue (there are even gradations between them). Exterior dialogue is what we generally think of when we compose a scene—two or more persons conversing (with drama, of course!) and moving the story forward. Interior monologue is one person conversing with himself (dramatically, naturally).

So, we can have something called interior monologue or stream of consciousness. It's interior because it's all in the character's head; there's no one else to bounce comments off, and some writers—notably James Joyce, Virginia Woolf and Marcel Proust—fashioned it into an extraordinary art form. For them, the interior monologue should mirror the jumbled, syntax-disoriented thought waves that fly through our heads, and they expected the reader to float along with them, picking up reactions and sensations and a vague story line in the process. In literary stories this will work (and sometimes work exceedingly well), but when we pull it down to a level where action and suspense must blossom, we need greater structure and more attention to the developing plot. Interior monologue *does* work with action and suspense, but Anthony Trollope's advice still lives: The dialogue, the monologue, must advance the story; or it must develop character.

If it does neither, it has no business in the story. But when it does what it's supposed to do, it works well:

> . . . so you watch the target crouch behind the tree and you know he doesn't see you, and you don't flash on his pain when your bullet hits because you know you'd wince and then you'd feel sorry and then you'd forget why you're here and then you'd be dead.

Here's action in the form of interior monologue. Something is happening and it's tense and life threatening. There's no uncertainty, no doubt about who is involved and what's going to take place. The only question is building resolve to get it done.

Or how about this:

> . . . what do I know about boats, I'm a musician, there're some better, a lot worse, but boats are scary, and I hide in this closet they call a head, waiting for *something* to show while jazz riffs flow through my mind, and I *know* I don't belong here because boats can sink.

Here, we have the interior monologue showing us something about the character (a fear of boats and why), and we have it set against an atmosphere of suspense. Why suspense? Because the character is anxious, and we don't know how things will turn out. There's uncertainty about what the "something" is and about how the character will deal with it. We can't say it's action because nothing is actually happening, yet the conflict grows in the character's head, and as long as it *keeps* building, that's suspense, folks.

GESTURING

Many of us recall the movie bad guy leaning against a wall, hard faced, guarding a doorway that leads to the big boss. It's an image that burst upon us with the gangster films of the 1930s, and the menace is palpable. If we use our imaginations, we can hear the director saying to the scriptwriter, back then:

"I don't want the gun to bulge, that's what everyone sets up. Dammit, turn this guy fearful, scary!"

"Without words, then?" the writer asks.

"Would *you* walk past him?"

Something physical . . . the writer thinks. "Maybe . . . he could clean his nails."

"With a razor-sharp nail file," the director adds.

"No words."

"None," the director says.

And we have the menacing image of the gangster who waits and watches while performing, for us, an unexpected human ritual. The contrast is eye-catching, of course—brutal man and dainty act—but in a dialogue sense, it is a dramatic piece of business because it offers a message without a single word exchanged:

> There is restrained violence here, and we don't need to hear harsh words or a menacing tone of voice. The threat is apparent.

This is the gesture, and it is dialogue just as much as the spoken word. It communicates, it moves matters forward, it develops character. Here's Ernest Hemingway from "The Killers," his story of two thugs, Al and Max, waiting in a diner to execute a man coming in for his supper:

> "Hey Al," Max called, "bright boy wants to know what it's all about."
>
> "Why don't you tell him?" Al's voice came from the kitchen.
>
> "What do you think it's all about?"

"I don't know."
"What do you think?"
Max looked into the mirror all the time he was talking.
"I wouldn't say."

We know from an earlier paragraph that the mirror was on the back wall of the diner and Max was sitting at the counter. So we can conclude that Max was watching for their victim to appear. The gesture is Max looking into the mirror *while* he is talking, and it emphasizes what the characters are saying. They aren't in the diner on an empty quest; they are watchful, and they are experienced.

And the gesture highlights the suspense because it adds a dimension—the character is *doing* something as well as saying something and emotions are heightened (as we touched on in chapter one). The outcome is uncertain, as in all good suspense moments, and Max's watchful stare in the mirror points up his own anxiety at what might transpire.

One purpose of gesturing is to build up conflict and tension. Our gangster with the nail file or the thug watching the mirror portray this well—both expand the watchful, controlled violence that the professional killer possesses. Note, too, especially with our nail-file gangster, that there is some underplaying (subdued, seemingly innocent), and this, too, can add to the menace. But the fact that the threats embody more than words means the conflict vibrates, and when this happens, the action and suspense grow.

What kind of gestures work? Remember, gesturing is dialogue, so it must communicate and it must drive the story forward and/or develop character. If we want to build conflict, we could have:

- "You did this," he said, *pointing his finger* at her deformed ear . . .
- "Why? he asked, *stomping* on a slow-moving beetle.

Or, if conflict build-up isn't crucial:

- "Ah," he said, pulling the bowl to him and *rubbing his hands*.
- "Please," he said, *nodding* toward the empty seat.

Gesturing also breaks up the spoken dialogue and injects a change of pace. See how Hemingway did it with Max looking into the mirror. The physical act of looking is different from the talking that went before it, and this forces the reader to pay attention and not get lulled by passage after passage of spoken dialogue, though if we're doing our dialogue the right way, no passage would be dull, would it? Perhaps a more accurate explanation might be that the reader *could* lose some of the significance of the spoken dialogue if exposed to it without a break.

In addition, gesturing can be dramatic, and this is important: He *tapped* his foot . . . he *cracked* his knuckles . . . he *toyed* with his tie pin . . . she *fiddled* with her glasses . . . she *blinked* rapidly . . . she *rubbed* the back of her hand absently.

Take any of these gestures and place them in a story, and we'll have a character communicating with other characters.

And with us.

CHAPTER 6

BUILDING THROUGH MOOD AND ATMOSPHERE

ONE DAY A FRIEND of yours hands you a manuscript and asks you to read it.

The first thing you notice is it's not a short story but a dramatic script. For the theater.

"A play," you say.

"My first," she says.

You read it carefully. "It's good," you say and mean it.

"It'll be better when the actors do it on stage," she says. "When there's color and props and *an atmosphere.*"

You understand. A theater script can't provide all of that. Dialogue? Yes. Characterizations? Yes. But atmosphere?

Think back to dramatic scripts you've read. The stories had that incomplete feeling; they needed substance and fleshing out. The dialogue had nothing physical to play against; the characters had no arena in which to move about and little stage business to enhance the impact of their lines.

The stories needed atmosphere and mood so the audience could *feel* the words. It works the same way with literature. Action and suspense thrive on atmosphere and mood because the reader must be involved in order to enjoy the story. We need to help the reader get involved, and creating a proper atmosphere or mood is one way to do it. Suppose we

- stalked another with vengeance on our mind?
- searched for a cure to a child's slow disintegration?

The first is action oriented, the last is suspense oriented and each can be enhanced with some attention to building up atmosphere and mood. For example, with vengeance we'd want to show obsession and hate, so we'd have the characters *feeling* these emotions, uttering them, thinking them and we'd have physical reminders (such as photos or trinkets or letters) to kindle and rekindle the vengeance. One character might bear scars—physical ones—another might have nightmares, but the object is to add to the impact of the words.

Or take the child-cure scenario where we wish to build up the suspense. Here the atmosphere and mood would be desperation and impending tragedy, growing despair and frustration. To set up the atmosphere and mood, we could develop a contrast with another child who is healthy and high-spirited and a relationship where the healthy child learns more and more from the sick child; we could describe the sick child's symptoms in great detail, we could show the slow breakdown of the family as the child gets sicker and sicker. We could show the first signs of a cure . . . only it's not discerned by the family. All of these could build suspense in the story (because the final outcome is so uncertain) and do so by feeding the proper atmosphere and mood.

Many writers turn to physical description as a springboard to atmosphere and mood, and there's no doubt it can work well with certain stories. "During the whole of a dull, dark and soundless day in the autumn of the year, when the clouds hung oppressively low in the heavens. . . . " wrote Edgar Allan Poe to open his "The Fall of the House of Usher," and the melancholy, depressing mood is established and will hang on for the entire story.

And W. Somerset Maugham in "The Outstation" described an English colonial official dressing for dinner on a remote island in Malaysia:

> The only concession he made to the climate was to wear a white dinner-jacket; but otherwise, in a boiled shirt and a high collar, silk socks and patent-leather shoes, he dressed as formally as though he were dining at his club in Pall Mall.

Here, we know we're dealing with a class-conscious, patronizing, overbearing character. And in this atmosphere, we're ready to understand resentment, confusion and an ultimate clash of cultures.

These are physical dimensions to atmosphere and mood, and they can paint a background that will lend authenticity as well as sensitivity to what is happening. Think of Native American literature by Dee Brown or Leslie Marmon Silko, or African-American literature by John Edgar Wideman or John Williams or Alice Walker. These authors give us physical description that presents an atmosphere or a mood that builds story content, and they do it well enough so we know it's authentic and it rivets us. Then they add bits of characterization and dialogue that move matters still further.

But physical description may not be enough to hold our readers. There must be *involvement*, and sometimes it means we must delve into emotions and feelings. We must wrap our readers inside a cocoon of story identification, and sometimes the best way to do that is to use both physical description and emotional reaching-out. Never forget, readers want to be entertained, so we start with a leg up—the readers' inclination. Don't shortchange readers' desires, and don't shortchange their urge for full involvement; if they think you can do better and simply didn't bother, they'll walk away.

So here's the key: Think *vividly*! Remember chapter two where we looked at strong verbs and charged language? We use these techniques to spur atmosphere and mood. Instead of describing a woman's dress as "reddish-brown" call it "earth-toned"; instead of writing "she cried," say "she sobbed"; instead of referring to "a large train bearing down," write "a monstrous shadow of steel and iron roaring toward us."

Action sequences, particularly, need charged imagery because they work best when the reader is right in the middle of the scene. Make the conflict harsh and encompassing, and the action will build. Make the atmosphere vivid, and the suspense will grow, along with the intensity of the story.

And when we're finished, the reader will be eager for more.

ANTICIPATION AND DREAD

Remember those moments when we thought we couldn't wait for something, when the twisting, excruciating *pain* was unbearable? What did we do? We *suffered*, and we tried to find relief by focusing on something else, but until that succeeded, we suffered!

And way down inside that suffering there was something telling us it wasn't so bad, that actually we might be better for the suffering. Paying the price, so to speak. And there were those of us who could get hooked on the suffering because it might be exciting!

Well, translate this to the written page and think of readers and how they might react in a similiar situation. We establish a character and set up a scenario where a monstrous event could occur *if* the character isn't able to control or settle or deduce the situation. From the early stages we know what *could* happen (notice I write "could" not "will"—it's important that this be seen as conditional since uncertainty is crucial), and this develops both a sense of anticipation (I know it's going to happen, what can I do to protect myself?) and dread (if it happens, I'll die!).

Anticipation and dread. Two basics of suspense. But why are these so important? Because they depend on the reader's suffering (and the character's suffering, too), and this develops into atmosphere and mood. What we must do is:

- arrange things so that something severe could happen unless certain things are done (anticipation), or
- have severe things happen and make it plain that other, even more severe things could happen (dread).

That idea of reader suffering actually takes the form of punishment when put into our writing hands. We are punishing our readers by making them suffer through our development of circumstances, which causes anticipation and dread. And we shouldn't apologize for doing this because it's what they really want: drama, excitement, uncertainty, unsettledness, fear and dread!

Good suspense writing can offer these things (it can also occur with action writing, but the atmosphere and mood tend to be direct, and the reader suffers less, though the characters probably suffer more).

For example, let's take a severe consequence: the poisoning of a major city's water system. With anticipation, the story revolves about whether the poisoning will take place and the efforts undertaken to prevent it. The suspense is in the question: Will it happen?

The atmosphere and mood develop through the conflict that springs from those who want to poison the water system and those who want to prevent it. The reader *anticipates* the horror if the water system is poisoned, and thus suffers through uncertainty until matters are resolved. We build that sense of anticipation by focusing on the possible consequences, by laying them out again and again so the reader *anticipates and suffers*.

With dread, the water system poisoning has already taken place (the severe thing that has happened), and now the question is how many will be killed, what will happen to the city's population (the more severe thing that could happen)? The reader must come to *dread* what will take place, and as with anticipation, we must focus on this, build up these severe consequences so the reader's sense of dread is full blown. Dread becomes atmosphere and mood because the reader doesn't know what will really happen! That pulsing uncertainty is the spur that keeps the level of dread high.

There is no better example of how this works than in Franz Kafka's *The Trial* (Knopf), where nothing appears to be as it should and where the lead character's frustration and bewilderment soon become the reader's. It begins with anticipation, and this is the opening line:

Someone must have traduced Joseph K., for without having done anything wrong, he was arrested one fine morning . . .

So, we assume he will battle to free himself, and we anticipate he will seek witnesses and prove to the authorities that he is innocent. Isn't that what all wrongly accused people do?

But then bizarre circumstances occur: Joseph K. is not informed of what he's done; he's ordered to appear for interrogation but not told when or where; he goes from one court to the next, unsure which has jurisdiction over him; and he meets a variety of people who offer him help, but none of them really do. The best advice he gets is to prolong the inquiry, avoid a decision, adjust to living forever on trial. In fact, we come to the realization that he will never be able to mount a defense.

And at this point our anticipation becomes dread, because now we realize that he's caught in an irrational system from which there appears to be no escape (and the suspense mounts). It's a recurring nightmare for any of us who see the world in rational terms, that irrational power over us cannot be neutralized or overcome. We become powerless in the face of it.

And so our sense of dread is now full blown. Severe things have happened: Joseph K. has been wrongly arrested and can mount no defense. More severe things could happen: He will finally succumb to the authorities.

That's what occurs. On the final page, two strangers appear, take him away and execute him.

And he never knows what crime he committed. We're left to wade through an atmosphere and mood of darkness and foreboding, a sense that life is merely a trick played on those of us who believe there is rational purpose in our existence.

It's not a happy view of things, but that's the way dread works sometimes. The point is to create it so that suspense can flower.

And then it's up to us to decide whether we wish to neutralize the dread (as Stephen King or Edgar Allan Poe might) or to let it hang, as Franz Kafka did. Either way, it develops atmosphere and mood, which kick in the suspense.

STEP BY STEP

I recall a newspaper story about two drivers involved in a fender-bender that ended with one of them dead and the other seriously wounded. They had never laid eyes on one another before, and neither was under the influence of drugs or alcohol. What happened was a classic tale of misunderstanding begetting more misunderstanding, challenge begetting more challenge, until both had painted themselves into corners of masculine pride. It reminded me of that childhood game where we piled weights on an upright pole, the object being to avoid adding the one weight that would cause things to come crashing down. Here, the drivers kept adding weights to the controversy over the accident until one of them said something too much, and the violence broke out.

It's a good scenario for action or suspense because conflict is present from the beginning. Conflict, in fact, is key because it's the fuel that stokes the flames of controversy ever higher. Step by step the antagonisms grow, and with each step, conflict flares anew. See how it might begin:

"Don't look too bad," Davy said, running his fingers across the Volvo's fender. "Not too bad."

"I dunno," Martin replied. "Look here, the door. Big dent."

"I was just crawlin' along."

"My wife yelled . . ."

"No stop sign neither, no way to tell nothin'."

"My brother's car, you know?" Martin tapped the caved-in door. "Who's gonna tell him?"

In six dialogue passages we have conflict well-positioned, but there's little intimation things will escalate. Martin is obviously distressed about the accident and the fact that the car doesn't belong to him. Davy tends to shrug matters off, which will have the effect of annoying and then antagonizing Martin. The step-by-step growth of this antagonism is the atmosphere and mood we wish to create—that is, the conflict develops burgeoning uncertainty, excitement and foreboding, and as the confrontation escalates, so does the drama. Matters might progress to:

"Someone get the cops!" Martin yelled to the small throng that had gathered. "This guy's crazy!"

Davy waved the tire iron. "You think you got dents? You got nothin'." He reared back and smashed the back window. "Now what, hotshot."

Martin shoved him away. "My brother . . . look at his car! You're . . ."

But Davy methodically smashed both taillights. *Whump! . . . scrrrunchhh . . .*

"The cops," Martin yelled. "Call the cops!"

Now matters have escalated. Step by step the confrontation has grown, from slight distress to full-blown battle. And the atmosphere and mood become more charged as a result. Along with the blossoming atmosphere and mood come the building action and suspense. Both are present here—action in the form of violence these two men inflict on each other, suspense in the form of uncertainty about the outcome. Will both survive? Will matters calm down? Will Martin be able to explain the car's damage to his brother?

Why does a step-by-step build-up work so well with action and suspense? Conflict's the answer. Each step in atmosphere and mood build-up adds (or should add) to the conflict, making it more dynamic, more imposing. And this, in turn, creates more interest in the story. The escalation carries us along, intrigued at where the confrontation might end.

Because we really don't know. Step by step we move, ever more conscious of the build-up; suspense and action grow, and the atmosphere and mood become more tightly drawn, more significant. Our uncertainties abound because we wonder what the outcome will be.

And then, of course, comes the climax.

But what if we already knew how the tale was going to end? Could that destroy the atmosphere and mood and draw down the action and suspense?

Consider Frederick Forsyth's *The Day of the Jackal* (Viking Press), set in the early 1960s during the French presidency of Charles de Gaulle. De Gaulle has granted independence to Algeria, but a violent French minority wants to reverse his policy. And they decide to assassinate him, hiring an international killer—the Jackal—on whom there is no known file. The book details the Jackal's step-by-step preparations for the assassination (and his tracking by a colorless French policeman), and as the story unfolds we find ourselves gripped by the action and growing suspense—even though Charles de Gaulle never actually died by an assassin's bullet; history is clear on that.

So we know the ending of this story—that the Jackal will fail—even as we read the first few pages. But our interest doesn't flag. And the reason is this: The author's step-by-step delineation of the Jackal's preparations catches our interest *because we come to know him intimately, and we even find ourselves rooting for him!* We have a curiousity about how one person would go about preparing to kill another, especially when that other is a chief of state, even though we, ourselves, would never think of doing it. And it doesn't matter that the Jackal failed; the fact remains he tried, and that's fascinating enough if the author describes his steps in sufficient detail and offers some insights we would never have expected.

For example, what would be the first step you or I would take, once we accepted the assignment? Become familiar with the target, probably. Forsyth has the Jackal go to the reading room of the British Museum and devour clips on de Gaulle, immersing himself in the man's character, habits, way of life. His target becomes a study, and in this we see the action and suspense begin to build, because we know the studying will be used for nefarious purposes. The atmosphere and mood become charged now, and the Jackal takes further steps in his preparation—arranging for four false sets of identity papers, for forged passports, for a special rifle that can be uniquely concealed. As his path takes him closer and closer to de Gaulle, we see him killing to preserve his concealed identity (while the French detective continues to track him), and the story becomes a chase: the Jackal after de Gaulle, the French detective after the Jackal. Step by step the story moves toward a climax, and the atmosphere and mood grow more tense and fearful. Even though we know the Jackal will not succeed, we're riveted by our intimate knowledge of him and by the action and suspense that have built up since the beginning of the book. With each step in his preparations, the Jackal has brought himself closer to de Gaulle, and this makes the suspense grow more severe, which, in turn, makes the action more dramatic because by now we're certainly part of the story (through our identification with the character).

We feel what's happening, we sympathize and understand. And it's because we've come to know that character so well.

But it's more than just familiarity with a character that's important. If we're going to use a step-by-step build-up in atmosphere and mood, we must remember to:

- plan it carefully. Pace it so that each step logically leads to the next.
- keep the steps relatively small, no big leaps.
- be certain of the atmosphere or mood we wish to achieve (fear, terror, disdain, depression, excitement, confusion). Understand how characters and circumstances are affected.
- think of specific ways to present it (physical description, emotions, special words, phrases and sounds).

And, above all, maintain the conflict.

PHYSICAL DESCRIPTION PLUS

There's little doubt that physical description alone (a table of food, furnishings in a house, the way a person dresses) can paint an atmosphere or a mood because it appeals to a recognizable something in us all. That physical description reminds readers of an event or spectacle or view they once experienced, and while certainly not identical to what's on the page, the memory will trigger an emotional response that sets an atmosphere or mood. For example, a table "laden with juicy hams and sausages surrounded by tall wedges of creamy cheeses and bunches of dewy-fresh grapes, apples and plums" will spark a feeling of hunger, perhaps even a remembered feast, and this, in turn, will set up an atmosphere of yearning and desire.

On the other hand, if we wrote, "there were blackened

bread crusts and dried milk stains amidst a gob of gelatinous cereal," we'd lose our hunger fast, especially if an unpleasant memory was sparked! There'd be no yearning either, and more likely, the atmosphere would evoke disgust or distaste.

Either way, the physical description has triggered a remembered something, and an atmosphere or mood has been created. Yearning on the one hand, distaste on the other, but by building this atmosphere or mood, we have set up possibilities for action and suspense.

If it's yearning, we have natural conflict — there's the yearner and the yearn-ee, and they don't see eye-to-eye. One wants what the other has, and the natural result is conflict. How do we express that conflict? Through action and/or suspense.

If action, the yearner takes the goodies and then tries to keep them.

If suspense, the yearner plots to take, and we are caught up in whether he will succeed or not.

Suppose it's distaste. Here again we have natural conflict — for example, squalid living versus a desire for something better. One can be satisfied with squalor or one can seek to get away from it. Either way, the conflict erupts (in both cases it's between the characters and their environment), and once again it's expressed through action and suspense.

If action, the character confronts, challenges and does battle with those who seek to prevent him from doing what he wishes (whether it's to remain in squalor or to escape it).

If suspense, the character isn't sure who the enemy is but knows there's someone or something, and we are caught up in his search to find out.

Simple physical description can be a prime atmosphere and mood setter because readers can "see" the object or the person the writer is describing (assuming, of course, the writer does the description well enough). The impact of that description determines the readers' feelings for what they read. A house that's sparsely furnished, for example, with colorless wallpaper and bare wood floors could show a sterile atmosphere that carries over to the characters. Who would live in such a house? People with sterile emotions who cared little for others. The reader picks that up, and now there's a sense of how the story is proceeding. Inject conflict, and we have a platform where either action or suspense can be involved.

And it's because the atmosphere was developed carefully.

What's happening is that the physical description appeals to the reader's emotions, and these emotions portray atmosphere or mood, which, in turn, develops action and suspense. But there's another way to achieve the same thing, and that's by appealing to one or more of our physical senses — touch, taste, smell, sight, hearing — without physical description. It's true that when we use physical description we seek to touch the reader's senses in order to produce emotion (think of that well-laden table and how the physical description made our mouths water; we felt hunger, which became yearning, which is emotion). But we don't always need physical description in order to show atmosphere and mood. Here is where the appeal to the senses comes in. Dialogue is one good way to do it:

"Oh," she said, "you're hurting . . ."

"The boy's name, tell it to me," he said softly. Then whispered. "I'm good at this, you know."

"My arm . . . I don't know, please, please . . . Oh!"

"Pity," he said, "bones can be so brittle."

The sense of touch is brought out here, and note there is no physical description to develop the atmosphere. But we feel the fear and the danger, and that's a strong influence on what the reader will feel, because if the characters feel it, the reader should be able to feel it, too. And as we develop that feeling, the action and suspense should build.

Try the sense of smell:

As he held her frail body, he noted the sourness in her breath. "Mary? Did you eat or drink anything?"

A harsh odor, curdling. "Only from the medicine bottle," she whispered.

"Where is it?"

> She licked her lips. The sourness again. "I f-finished it. . . ."

Can't we smell what's in that bottle? Don't we sense the ominous situation developing? There's no physical description here, only an appeal to the reader's sense of smell, which will then develop the emotion of fear and uncertainty.

Which becomes the atmosphere of danger.

And we could move the story forward with action or suspense because we've established our atmosphere and mood.

Why does an appeal to the senses work so well? It gets our readers *involved* by having them feel what the characters are feeling (that writer-reader partnership, remember?). Readers empathize and identify, and the atmosphere envelops the story.

It works best when we're specific about those sense appeals. Use details and more details, don't be content with vague generalities such as "the dark night made everyone feel afraid." Instead, write:

> Black mist ran up our nostrils, we could smell the sour sea; the darkness showered us with its ominous power, we could taste the tainted salt.

Specifics give us a handle to grasp as the writer portrays emotions by developing a sense appeal. The more specific the images, the more thoroughly the reader will feel them, and that, of course, is what we writers seek. Think of it like building a ladder: We have to place the rungs close enough and often enough so there's no misstep and no confusion. The more specific we are about the senses we wish to develop, the more rungs — *details* — there will be, and the more fully the senses will come alive.

So we use strong emotions, strong feelings when action and suspense are the goal. The greater the emotions, the more dynamic the action and the more affecting the suspense. Don't be afraid to take the restraints off.

And you'll pat yourself on the back for the atmosphere and mood you've created.

CHAPTER 7

BUILDING THROUGH CHARACTER DEVELOPMENT

AS THE LATE EDITOR William Sloane put it, "Fiction is people." It's written *for* people, it's made up *of* people, and it's written *by* people. In his fine handbook *The Craft of Writing* (Norton), he says:

> People—characters—are the true substance of all fiction, most nonfiction, all drama, and a lot of poetry ranging from the *Iliad* to Robert Lowell. . . . There is no such entity as a piece of fiction that is devoid of human beings. . . . People *are* the story and the whole story.

This is so true with action and suspense because the reader must identify with the story and become a part of it. If the characters aren't believable or don't excite interest, the reader closes the book with a resounding thud!

Borriinng. Put that writer on the Don't-Pick-Up-Again list.

It doesn't matter whether it's fiction or nonfiction, people—characters—are where we begin. We must think *people* first! Who, instead of why or where or how, because *who* is the engine that drives the story.

Think of Hercule Poirot, Agatha Christie's famous detective. Without his closely drawn character, many of her mysteries could not have been pieced together. Or think of Pilar and Maria and Robert Jordan in Ernest Hemingway's *For Whom the Bell Tolls*. Their diverse characters set the story tone and drive it forward. Or think of Maxim de Winter in Daphne du Maurier's

Rebecca. Without his smoldering presence the story would not have depth or suspense.

These writers sculpt characters around whom they build a story. They make characters more than one dimensional, giving them flesh and blood so they can carry the story.

How's it done? Think *memorable*. A character should be *memorable*. Different, unusual, arresting. Not the entire person, either; it might be one characteristic only (an angry scar running from eyebrow to chin, a womanly voice in a man with the build of a weight lifter. These are what stick in a reader's mind. It's much easier if there is something out of the ordinary about the character, something the reader won't forget.

It doesn't have to be physical, of course; it could be emotional. Think of Richard Condon's *The Manchurian Candidate* (McGraw-Hill) where Raymond Shaw is programmed to kill when an outside stimulus is presented. Until that occurs, he's as normal as the rest of us. The point is that this character is memorable because he has a single bizarre characteristic, and we wonder if and when it will erupt.

Besides the suspense aspects (which are in great supply here), we have someone the reader will clearly fix on. Richard Condon has done his work well; Raymond Shaw is unique and bizarre and *memorable*.

Developing a character like this is one way to build action and suspense. In making a character memorable, we set up opportunities for conflict because one outsized characteristic requires another contrasting one. For example, with a woman who is six-foot-six it's not hard to imagine the intimidation many men would feel, especially if she carries her height well and moves with self-confidence. The men might challenge her repeatedly, trying to mute the intimidation.

Or how about the man with the ugly scar? Fear might be his message, and others might see him as a danger. Conflict would be the natural outgrowth. It's what the memorable characteristic presents to other characters that is the key — is it a challenge, *should* it be a challenge?

If it is, we have conflict. And as the character develops, so do the action and suspense.

Consider this: a character at war with himself (such as Raskolnikov in Dostoevsky's *Crime and Punishment*). He has a memorable characteristic (a moral righteousness to murder someone he feels is his inferior). The conflict's quite clear (should he confess to a killing, will he get away with it), and the action and suspense proceed. As Raskolnikov becomes more concerned he will be found out, we see the police investigation grow closer and closer, and the action and suspense increase. Raskolnikov's memorable characteristic has produced the inevitable conflict, as it should, and we have a story centered upon a character whose human traits drive things along.

Make those characters memorable (Remember: Most writing, fiction as well as nonfiction, is *people*), and the conflict as well as the action and suspense will spread themselves like an open fan. Think of characters at war—either with themselves or with others—and then chronicle that war until there is peace.

MULTIPLE FACES

As we go about building a character, we touch on different sides of that character's personality. We want to avoid the cardboard cutout, the single-dimension character because the reader, unless the plot is extremely powerful, will have trouble staying interested in the story.

So we explore the character, bringing out those things that are exciting, unnerving, *memorable*. Multidimensional.

What about a couple of personalities *within* the same body? Talk about multidimensional. Here's a character with more than one face, and doesn't that make for interesting possibilities?

Conflict right off the bat. The different personalities at war with one another. The classic, of course, is Robert Louis Stevenson's *The Strange Case of Dr. Jekyll and Mr. Hyde*, in which a kindly doctor and a malevolent criminal occupy the same body, and the story swings between their attempts to gain control of the overall personality. Here's the way Edward Hyde is described by one of the other characters:

"[He] was pale and dwarfish, he gave an impression of deformity without any nameable malformation, he had a displeasing smile . . . and he spoke with a husky, whispering and somewhat broken voice."

Then, a few pages later, here is the way Dr. Jekyll is described:

. . . a large, well-made, smoothfaced man of fifty, with something of a slyish cast, perhaps, but every mark of capacity and kindness.

Two different personalities living within the same body, one dwarfish, the other large; one malformed, the other well-made; one sinister, the other open. Conflict after conflict.

And isn't this a recipe for burgeoning action and suspense? As the conflicts appear, the action and the suspense develop. The struggle between the two personalities is action oriented because Hyde engages in criminal act after criminal act, and we shudder at the character's thirst for evil. What he does is described mostly by others after the fact, but that does nothing to minimize the viciousness, and with each murder or assault we wonder how he can be stopped.

And this is where the suspense comes in. We know that uncertainty is the basis of suspense, so the question is, where's that uncertainty? There's no doubt Hyde committed the crimes, and when they're described, that's action (things happen—no uncertainty there). But even though we know who did what, we don't know who will prevail in the end! We don't know whether Jekyll will succeed in cleansing himself of Hyde, or whether Hyde will take over Jekyll entirely. This is the suspense, the uncertainty: *Who will prevail?*

In a body with multiple faces it's a most dramatic question. And it provides an excellent chance to portray both action and suspense. Remember conflict. Think conflict *first*. Get those multiple faces to stick their tongues out at one another.

Then build the action and the suspense, as the distinctions between the personalities grow more severe and ominous.

Sometimes the multiple-faces approach can take a bizarre

twist. Suppose a character wishes to remain forever young, never to grow old or whither. He wants to stand nature on its head. No multiple faces here, right? One man, one desire, one personality.

But what if . . . his valued portrait begins to show age signs even as he stays young? This, of course, is the story in Oscar Wilde's *The Picture of Dorian Gray*. The conflict comes between the character, Dorian Gray, and his portrait. The man remains young, the portrait ages. Still multiple faces, just different because one is within the human body and the other is outside of it. But the faces are in conflict, and this is a springboard for action (hiding the portrait, making excuses for it, deciding to destroy it) and suspense (what will happen when the portrait is seen or destroyed?). Wilde builds his character by showing an ever-more dissolute Dorian Gray thumbing his nose at nature, secure that his youth will be perpetual, and as the character builds so do the action and the suspense.

And how about the story of Superman? Or of other cartoon characters hiding one personality within the body of another? Superman and Clark Kent, there's a conflict for you. Mild-mannered reporter (I'm not above clichés when they serve a purpose) versus Mr. Everything! It isn't Jekyll and Hyde, at war with one another, but the personalities are opposites, though control is fully with Mr. Everything. He decides when to be Clark Kent, when to be Superman, and suspense comes when he must decide to hide one or the other personality. Action abounds, too, especially when Superman makes his appearance and strives to rein in the bad guys.

But note the suspense, as well. There's some concern over whether Superman will prevail, but mainly the suspense is in the *hiding* of the dual personalities from others. How can Clark Kent continue to hide his Superman persona, will he be found out? How can Superman hide his Clark Kent persona? If the conflict between the two personalities wasn't present, chances are the suspense wouldn't be there either.

When dealing with multiple faces, remember this: Put those faces in conflict and watch the action and suspense pour out.

TERRIBLE SECRETS

I recall a writing teacher discussing the germ of a story idea. Someone had wondered, in that way many students do, "What do I start with?"

Not how do I start but what do I start *with*?

The teacher looked us over and asked a simple question. "How many of you have a secret you've never shared with a single living soul?"

Most of us raised our hands.

"How many of you would feel comfortable with writing about it?"

No one raised their hand.

"Good," he nodded. "That means it's a secret with punch. And *that* means it would make the germ of a good story."

He went on to say he didn't insist we write about our deeply held secrets, only that we understand such things are what churn out an arresting tale. "All of us have secrets," he said. "Most of us have at least one we couldn't share with others because it would be too frightening, too embarrassing, too hurtful, too dangerous. Building a story around secrets like this is a neat way to go."

He called it *finding the terrible secret*, and over the years I've seen it applied again and again with fiction and nonfiction. It jump-starts the story like few things do.

It should be character-oriented; that is, it should be something that one or more persons hold closely, guard jealously, and it should involve *them*; it should not be "quest-oriented" in the sense that the secret becomes a prize to be sought. And don't forget it must be *terrible*; it must be a hell-on-earth for the person or persons who guard the secret. They must be willing to go to great length — perhaps even at the cost of their own life — to protect the secret.

And why does this work so well with action and suspense? Conflict, once again. The terrible secret, divulged or not, produces essential conflict *because it is so terrible*. Other characters are or would be repelled, some would feel betrayed or seriously harmed. The terrible secret produces conflict in the way a strong wind whips the surface of a mill pond. It is inevitable.

So we begin with a character or characters who have a terrible secret. And then we slide into action or suspense, depending upon whether we want the secret to be divulged right away (in which case we'd have action because things would start to happen) or not divulged (in which case we'd have suspense because there would be uncertainty about what would happen *when* it is divulged).

How does it work? Take a look at Leon Uris's *QB VII* (Doubleday), the story of a libel trial in London, in which a writer has accused a prominent scientific researcher of performing medical experiments on Jewish concentration camp inmates in Poland during World War II. The researcher, Dr. Adam Kelno, a Polish national who became a British citizen after the war, has been knighted for his selfless work with the people of Borneo, which included developing food production procedures for allaying famine and protein deficiency. He has never denied working in a Nazi hospital, but he claims he tried to save lives and help people escape. But now comes the book with its cruel charge, and here is the crucial passage:

> In the notorious barrack V a secret surgery was run by Dr. Kelno, who carried out fifteen thousand or more experimental operations without the use of anesthetic.

Here is a terrible secret, and the character of Adam Kelno is the key to the book. Did he do it or didn't he? If he did, he's a monster; if he didn't, he's been greviously wronged. Either way, the secret colors the progress of the story, and we find ourselves going back and forth as the author builds Kelno's character.

Because it is Kelno's character that is at issue here! Since we don't know whether the charges are true until the end, this book is more in the suspense than the action camp (uncertainty, remember?), but that doesn't mean the conflict doesn't persevere. It hugs each page as the issue of Kelno's character is explored (did he do it or didn't he?), and the terrible secret keeps vibrating in its unanswered form until the final few pages.

If we think deeply enough, all of us can come up with a

terrible secret (our own or a fictional one), and then we can begin to see how a character will try to live with it. It could be sexual (incest, rape, child molestation) or political (espionage, betrayal, election stealing) or social (ancestor denial, HIV vulnerability, felony conviction) or something else. But it must be a *terrible* secret in order to have a major influence on the character and his way of life.

Do we let on about the secret at an early stage? After all, if our readers don't know the secret exists, how can they understand its terrible nature? So we answer with a yes and no. Yes, we should give out something about the secret early, though we needn't spell it out completely. But the reader has to suspect something isn't quite right, so there is sufficient foreshadowing when the secret comes to light later. No, we needn't offer a full description because that can wait until it does the most good.

Until, in other words, the suspense is at the breaking point. Take a look at Len Deighton's *Berlin Game* (Knopf), in which the protagonist, Bernard Samson, and his wife, Fiona, both work in British intelligence during the height of the Cold War. Bernard has been trying to encourage an east bloc agent to defect, and he has spent considerable time in East Germany for that specific purpose. As the situation grows more tense, we see the relationship between Bernard and Fiona strain because of Bernard's absences and Fiona's cavalier attitude toward him. It's obvious Fiona is a bit bored, though she continues to do her work at London headquarters—until one day she disappears!

And a day or two later she turns up in East Berlin, alone, working for the east bloc. She has been their person-in-place within British Intelligence for years, and this has been her terrible secret. She grew up in British society, attended the best schools, married well, had two children, and now she is a turncoat spy.

It is a terrible secret that the author doesn't divulge until the end of the book, but we get little hints that she is preparing to defect. Her attitude toward husband and children grows less intimate, she is out of touch for brief periods (something that never happened before), the east bloc seems unusually confident about *something* to do with Germany.

If we read the book carefully, we can sense these hints, even as we follow the underlying story of Bernard and his own east-bloc defector. Fiona's terrible secret is a conflict-maker if I ever saw one, even though we don't get its full flavor until the end. But the hints of her ultimate defection and the certainty that all is not well between Bernard and Fiona provide enough tension so we can't help but wonder what will come next . . . or how the story will end.

When the terrible secret finally is revealed, we lean back, nod and say, of course, *that's* where it was all leading!

And isn't she a monster for leaving her husband and children behind?

INEVITABLE COLLISIONS

One of Alfred Hitchcock's most useful techniques was to take innocent characters and put them into a bizarre situation. "To see how they'd react," Hitchcock was reported to have chortled, but, of course, there was more to it than that. Hitchcock was setting up an immediate conflict by mixing inappropriate characters and events, and then the characters would have to get by — somehow. Hitchcock often began by developing the characters in their own world and then switching to the unfolding event, which, at this time, hadn't affected the characters. Back and forth he would go, and each time the characters and the event would come closer and closer together until. . . .

Bang! Smash! Ugh! Characters and events ran into one another. It was the inevitable collision (inevitable because we knew, simply *knew*, it would happen), and it was a collision because the characters were unsuspecting and the event was *there*.

This is a welcome story writing technique because some of the work is already done for you. Here's what you need:

- two characters or one character and an event
- neither ever involved with the other
- if two characters, they need not be opposites, but they should hold differing values

- if a character and an event, one should be totally unprepared for the other
- the collision should produce sparks

What's already done for you is that the conflict is built in. You set up the characters and/or the event, and by following the guidelines above, you have automatic conflict.

And it can work its way to action or suspense. Suppose, for example, there's a young boy, orphaned and a victim of civil war in his strife-torn African country; he wanders alone, bewildered, through the bush seeking only shelter and food to see him through the day. Now suppose there's a middle-aged American woman, a cancer victim who has been in remission for six months; she is determined to spend her late husband's money traveling the world in the time left to her. She is bitter, resentful, self-centered, and on photo-safari in Africa she finds everything dirty, unpleasant and uncomfortable.

Isn't this the recipe for a story? As we flip from the young boy to the woman and back again, we know they will meet, and we know there will be the inevitable collision. A collision because the boy stands for what the woman despises, and the woman becomes a means of survival for the boy. As we develop the characterizations, we begin to understand the points of collision, and we see the characters drawn closer and closer together until the sparks fly!

The inevitable-collision story is especially good with mystery-suspense work because we can feel the suspense build as the characters (or the character and the event, such as a building storm or a spreading plague or a massacre) move toward one another. The further we separate the characters on the page, the more we'll have to work with as the inevitable collision awaits. It works the same way as the need for confrontation we discussed in chapter one. Drama builds, and excitement grows.

Remember, the reader wants to understand. A collision that doesn't have the sense of inevitability is really only a contrivance. Take it slow and easy, back and forth, step-by-step, moving ever closer, highlighting the points of conflict between the characters or between a character and the event. Then . . .

Bam! Smash! Ugh! Collision time.

And we knew it would happen all the time, didn't we?

INEVITABLE CHOICES

One of the ways we keep characters from stagnating is by putting them into situations in which they must make choices. Not life-and-death situations necessarily, but choices which will have an effect on their lives. Think of Huckleberry Finn and his decision to have Jim, the fugitive slave, join him on his raft journey down the Mississippi. Or Philip Carey's decision (made several times) to remain with Mildred even though she treats him with disdain in W. Somerset Maugham's *Of Human Bondage*. These decisions altered lives and gave the characters depth and scope. They also set up the groundwork for action and suspense, because the choices, themselves, were conflict-laden.

When a character faces a major choice, there's usually conflict because the choice is not easy. Do I do it, don't I do it? As the character goes back and forth, the conflict follows because if the choice was easy, the character would have little doubt, and there would be no drama in the choice-making. So, we make the choice difficult, and the character has to agonize over.

Conflict settles in, and the next question is to decide how long we want the agony to persist. Each time we highlight the choice (characterize it, dramatize it), we are highlighting the conflict also, so we may wish that conflict to run for a while. But at some point the choice has to be made, and if we've been doing a decent job of developing our characters, the choices they make should be appropriate. That is, we should nod and say, "Of course!" as the choice is made.

What kind of choices can these be? Think of them as options, as ways of resolving dilemmas within categories.

- The *money* option: to sell the family farm to a developer
- The *revenge* option: to get even with one who has injured you

- The *obligation* option: to pursue a quest because a personal debt is owed
- The *adventure* option: to seek a brand-new experience
- The *peace of mind* option: to resolve uncertainties and threats against you, even if it's painful

I don't presume to exhaust the list of options, but these will give you a jump-start on coming up with inevitable choices. These can translate into action and/or suspense because, of course, the conflict is right there, in the option, from the beginning.

Let's look at that word *inevitable*. Many would think it means that the ultimate choice is preordained, that it's the only possible alternative. Not so. Inevitable refers not to which choice must be made but to the fact that *some* choice must be made. The character must choose because the circumstances of the story dictate it, but what that choice will be isn't inevitable.

Let's look at the peace-of-mind option and see how it plays out in Tom Wolfe's *Bonfire of the Vanities* (Farrar, Straus, Giroux). Sherman McCoy, millionaire bond trader, Park Avenue resident, husband and father, was in a hit-and-run accident while his girlfriend was driving his car. At first he has little apprehension because, of course, *she* was driving. He even suggests they call the police who, at this point, have no idea of his identity. But his girlfriend restrains him:

> "Sherman, if we tell 'em the truth, they're gonna *kill* us. You understand that?" . . . You were driving, thought Sherman. Don't forget that part. It reassured him. . . .

At this point the inevitable choices blossom: He can call the police and make a clean breast of it, hide the crime, take the responsibility himself, or talk his girlfriend into taking responsibility (which would clear him). We don't know what he'll do, but we do know he'll have to make one of these choices because the story of the hit-and-run is building all around him. The newspapers have it, the district attorney feels pressure to solve the matter, television commentators and citizen organizers are urging the people to demand answers.

Then the police trace his license plate and come calling at his Park Avenue apartment. He denies his car was involved and refuses to allow them to examine it. They leave, but with their suspicions aroused.

There's no doubt he must make a choice now; the police aren't going to leave him alone. Note how the conflict walks in the footsteps of the choices, how each time Sherman comes face-to-face with his dilemma, the conflict is boosted. He decides he must find a tough criminal lawyer, even though there's been no indictment. The lawyer's office, his appearance and his conversation are much grittier than Sherman is used to, but:

> To his surprise, once he got started, Sherman found it easy to tell his story in this place, to this man. Like a priest, his confessor, this dandy with a fighter's nose, was from another order.

And so Sherman has made his choice, he has told all and now awaits his fate. No longer does he hide what he did, nor does he attempt to protect his girlfriend. That he would have to make some kind of choice was apparent from the beginning, and the major suspense was in waiting to see which choice it would be. So he took the peace-of-mind option and settled one thing, at least momentarily.

Because the next step will show what happens to him in court. And here conflict arises again and suspense and action bloom: action because things will be *happening* in that courtroom (spurred by ever-present conflict) and suspense because we really don't know how he'll fare at the hands of judge and jury until the end.

But by this time the inevitable choices have already been made, and the character of Sherman McCoy is fully drawn. The drama of his decision is what has kept our attention, and while we may find him disagreeable, we certainly couldn't find his situation dull.

Which, of course, is why we create inevitable choices in the first place.

CHAPTER 8

BUILDING THROUGH POINT OF VIEW

IN EVERY WRITING COURSE there's a time when the business of the writer's eye comes up. I don't mean physiologically but figuratively, as in "Through whose eye is this story or chapter or section being told?"

"Whose means of perception?"

"Whose point of view?"

Every story—fiction as well as nonfiction—is made up of points of view or *character slants*. It's the way the character—or characters—perceive the world under the limitations arranged by the writer.

"I saw the lion attack the man," gives a different character slant than "He saw the lion attack the man," and that difference is much more than a simple change in sentence subject. It allows us as writers greater or lesser latitude to do what we wish with the character or characters.

As we discussed in chapter two, the "I" signifies that the writer is inside the character's head, and whatever that character perceives is limited by that fact. "I saw the lion" means the writer is using the *first-person singular*, and if there was another lion attack somewhere outside the character's field of perception, the character couldn't describe it *since he wasn't there to see it!*

"I" means the writer's—and the character's—eye is narrowly focused to what can be perceived by that first-person singular point of view.

"He saw the lion," on the other hand, broadens things because now we're into the third person, and this means of percep-

107

tion — called *third-person objective* — allows the writer to step back a bit and take a wider approach. (Remember, however, as mentioned earlier, we can use third person and still keep things narrow. It's called third-person *subjective* because the writer can limit the characters' means of perception — as with first person — and retain the third person. "He saw," "she thought," and the story revolves around what that character perceives. It's limited to that.) Using third-person objective, the writer can sit above the characters and manipulate them in different locations and at different times. It allows the writer to enter the head of any character and stay there for a while ("He thought . . . he wondered . . . he felt . . . he decided . . ."), but then to move away to another character and repeat the process.

Multiple or single points of view, however, should be seen for what they are — techniques, tools, crafts — as discussed in chapter two. They will shape a story in different ways, and one works better in certain circumstances, another works better elsewhere. First-person singular, for example, works well when the writer wants the reader to get close to and intimate with the character, and when that lead character is strong enough to carry the entire story; third-person objective or subjective works better when the story lends itself to multiple settings, and there might be several dominant characters (though a single dominant character would work, too).

But both points of view enhance conflict and are instrumental in developing action and suspense. With the "I" technique, the conflict remains inside the head of the lead character: "I saw the lion attack the man." That's conflict even though we're seeing things through the eyes of this one character. We don't need another point of view.

"He saw the lion attack the man" is conflict, too. But let's add another point of view:

> The man's scream caught Joan as she returned to the Land Rover for bug repellant. She could see nothing, but she knew it was bad, and she shivered, knowing Alec was out there somewhere.

By changing the point of view we've enlarged the canvas, and also added a layer of conflict—now it isn't only Alec who sees the man attacked and feels danger, but it's Joan who fears for Alec and also feels danger. As the means of perception changes, the opportunity for conflict and tension multiplies.

And the action and suspense build as the conflict develops because these items are always linked. As we've said before, there can be no action or suspense without conflict; it is in the nature of things that for a reader to be moved by action or suspense sequences, there must be conflict at the core.

Action sequences: a crime, a chase, an athletic contest, a fight for survival.

Suspense sequences: unexplained disruptions, anxiety, prolonged pain.

Each of these needs conflict to become part of a story. And the point of view we use adds or detracts from story impact.

Take a suspense sequence such as an unexplained disruption. What does an event like this generate among the characters? Curiosity, probably, followed by the attempt to relate it to themselves. Its significance in the story, however, depends upon the point of view of the character with whom we're dealing *at that moment.*

Suppose the unexplained disruption was a dent in the door of the family car, and no one was willing to admit knowing anything about it. If the story is in the "I" mode, this is really the only point of view we are concerned with:

> I was watching Jamie, and he never lost his half-smile, as Father asked each of us in turn. . . .

Of course, another character could offer views too, but such views would be extremely limited:

> "I haven't driven the thing in a week," said Jamie. "You ask me, I think Lois bumped it when she came home from that bank party the other night."

We don't know his motivation for saying this because we aren't inside his head, yet we do get another point of view, limited though it is. Note the conflict right from the start with first-person singular. The unexplained dent means that someone has done *something*. The protagonist can ruminate about this, weighing and judging the other characters and their motivations, but no other character can do it because of the point of view.

Now, let's use third-person singular with the same facts:

Harry watched Father ask each of them, in turn, about the dent. It was a throwback to when they were young, and he remembered how they had all shielded one another.

Then, let's shift point of view:

Bobby couldn't believe the way Jamie just grinned at Father, as if this was one big joke. Didn't he understand how Father felt about the car? Jamie never appreciated. . . .

Here, we're not limited by what's in only one character's head. We have two points of view and two *different* reactions to the same facts, but the conflict remains no matter which way we turn. And so does the suspense because we don't know at this point what Father will do about the dent or whether any of the characters will own up. Until that happens, things remain uncertain.

Which is exactly where good suspense should put us.

CONVERGING THEMES

Two points of view or one . . . three points of view or two . . . or one? Decisions that make us realize writing is work! *We* have to make a choice because the quality of our story could well depend on how we proceed. We have to think about whether a first-person singular point of view will hold the reader through several hundred pages of manuscript: Is the character strong for this, are we able to provide the *complete* story through the eyes of only one character? Perhaps we want to keep things intimate and burrow deeply into this single character's perceptions and experiences. Readers can be quick to identify with this approach because they *want* to be involved, and we're allowing them to put up a magnifying glass. Then, too, perhaps it's the kind of story where we feel more in control when a single point of view is followed. Matters do get complicated when we shift the point of view around, just like juggling two or three balls instead of tossing up only one.

We should make these point-of-view determinations while we're putting together our story outline. *Who* should tell the story, we ask ourselves, how many whos should there be? Is it the kind of story that develops in places and perceptions beyond the limited viewpoint of a single character? If so, we should move the point of view around.

An example: war stories such as Norman Mailer's *The Naked and the Dead* (Rinehart) or Philip Caputo's *A Rumor of War* (Holt, Rinehart and Winston) are noteworthy because they show the war's effects on a variety of people, and these effects wouldn't be so poignant if we only got a single character's point of view. By shifting viewpoints, the authors have broadened perspective and portrayed the intimate feelings of several characters. Ah, you're thinking, with first-person singular, others can relate how they feel to the person through whose eye the story is being told. True enough, but we aren't—can't be—*inside* the head of any other character, and this limits what the reader can perceive.

There are times, then, when we want to have multiple points of view through which we can develop quick-paced action and suspense along with a broadening story line. We know conflict can be easily portrayed with multiple points of view (think disagreement, think *differences*), and action and suspense can follow and build nicely. Among the most useful ways of employing multiple points of view is to develop two or more story themes and have the points of view mirror those themes.

Take any two ideas . . . a man in trouble at a supermarket checkout counter because he tried to steal food . . . a woman discussing with a psychotherapist whether to leave her husband.

These are two unrelated themes, yet each has a point of view, and if we could develop them as pillars of a story, we'd have a pretty good beginning.

The secret is to have the themes *converge*, have them move closer and closer to one another, have the points of view broaden and build until they embrace one another. It needn't be done in the course of a few pages; in fact, that would be rushing things. As we did with characterizations and "inevitable collisions" in chapter seven, here we do it with points of view: step-by-step, one little move after another, each theme becoming a story in itself until, finally, the two stories mesh. At this point, action and suspense have grown steadily, and now there is a climax that can create a new story with a new theme or it can stop right here. The choice would depend upon how many questions remain unanswered. Let's see how it might work:

1. *man at supermarket* — refuses to talk when arrested, his mind filled with resentments

2. *woman and therapist* — agonizes over leaving husband, but he bores her, and he's turning mean

3. *man* — lives in basement apartment, out of jail six months, no job, is totally depressed

4. *woman* — wants to work but husband says no, recently lost father, much better man than husband

5. *man* — supermarket manager sees public relations coup by not prosecuting and offering to find him a job, refuses to press charges

6. *woman* — announces divorce intentions to husband, he is livid, and she flees but begins looking for work

At this point there hasn't been much convergence. But let's move the story forward to where the man has grown to be a success in the supermarket business and is now being groomed for a major corporate position, though he remains burdened with feelings of inadequacy. And the woman has shed her husband (not without threatening moments) and just graduated from law school near the top of her class, though still unnerved whenever she sees her ex-husband.

1. *man* — discovers money laundering by top corporate executives, is torn between loyalty and ambition, writes anonymous letter to U.S. Attorney

2. *woman* — takes job with U.S. Attorney and is assigned to look into money laundering charges; finds ex-husband involved

Now, we have convergence, even though it may be some time before the man and the woman meet face-to-face. But the themes have converged by virtue of the U.S. Attorney connection. The story lines will slowly merge, and the points of view will move in lockstep, ever closer, ever more illuminating, until they become the same story.

These converging themes, highlighted by differing points of view, can be action or suspense oriented, of course, so long as they trace paths that will move toward one another. Take action, for example:

- *First theme*: A young man, recently released from prison, decides to become a prizefighter.
- *Second theme*: A retired military officer secretly trains a paramilitary group for political purposes.

At first, these themes seem to have nothing in common, yet the artful writer will use the element of violence to strike a common chord and slowly draw them together. Each theme, remember, is really a complete story with its own conflicts and plots and subplots, but as we go along, the two stories should begin to merge, and the points of view should begin to cross (how that happens I'll leave to your bubbling imagination).

Just remember: step-by-step, closer and closer.

Suppose we want to mix action and suspense themes? As we've mentioned, no story has to be all action or all suspense; we can have elements of both. Try this:

- *First theme*: Searchers are combing rugged terrain for campers who have disappeared; weather and wild animals make it hazardous.
- *Second theme*: A man and his wife seek spiritual redemption in a bizarre, sexual ritual.

What do these two themes have in common? The element of searching for something. And while the first theme is action-oriented, the second theme is more suspenseful. Can we bring the two themes, and their points of view, together? A little imagination should do it because the searches should cross paths at some point. They should converge.

And when they do, the stories merge into a whole, and the points of view now concentrate on the same elements. Different points of view, certainly, but observing the same scene.

And we never lost the conflict, did we?

YOUR VIEWPOINT OR MINE?

Regardless of whether we follow a single or multiple point of view, it's always easier to stay with one theme throughout a story, though it doesn't, necessarily, make the writing less arduous. What it can do is focus undivided attention on a single theme without the distraction of cutting away to become involved in something else altogether. It allows deeper penetration of motives, memories and mirages—the three *M*s (apologies to you know who):

- *Motives*: Why characters do what they do.
- *Memories*: What happened to make the characters do what they do.
- *Mirages*: How the characters fool themselves about what happened and why they did it.

Yet, limiting ourselves to a single theme doesn't mean we limit ourselves to a single point of view—there can be multiple points of view, as well. Here's where the hard work comes in, because in developing multiple points of view, we must develop multiple characterizations. Each viewpoint means a characterization in some form:

He watched them raise the manhole cover, and now the bomb trigger was set. In a matter of seconds. . . .

or

She shuddered to see the manhole cover raise. Nightmares from her youth dictated a monster from the sewers would emerge.

Two different people viewing the same event: the man as a criminal, the woman as a frightened bystander. But note that we've characterized them, and that *by virtue of these characterizations* they can look at the same event and come away with different reactions.

Two different viewpoints, same facts.

We build action and suspense this way; what one person perceives, another might not, and when these perceptions—or lack of them—are in conflict, there's a story to write. See how Mary Higgins Clark does it in *Loves Music, Loves to Dance* (Simon & Schuster), in which two young women, close friends, move to New York and begin exciting careers. Nona, a television producer, wants to do a documentary on the kind of people who place personal get-together ads, and the two young women agree to help. And one of them, Erin Kelley, gets killed. Research for the documentary goes forward, and now Nona and her assistant, Liz Kroll, are planning which interviews to use and in what order. Liz finishes with:

> " . . . If your friend Erin Kelley had actually met her date that night, we'd have a heck of a terrific wrap-up."
>
> "Wouldn't we ever," Nona said quietly, and realized that she had never liked Liz.
>
> Kroll did not seem to notice. "That FBI agent, Vince D'Ambrosio, is cute. I talked to him yesterday."

They are both focused on the same event, the planning of the documentary, and they both touch on the death of Erin Kelley. But here's where their points of view differ: Nona offers sarcasm, and an instant of sadness, as she realizes she never has liked Liz. Liz is insensitive and doesn't realize she has offended Nona, nor does she catch the fact that Nona doesn't like her.

Instead, after her insensitive remark about Erin Kelley, she flits to a gossipy comment about a man.

One event here, two viewpoints and some characterization:

- *Nona*: sarcastic, saddened, doesn't like Liz
- *Liz*: insensitive, gossipy, opportunistic

It's more suspense than action because people are talking rather than *doing* things, but the conflict in the points of view makes it intriguing for the reader to continue. How will this dislike and insensitivity play later on, when the story has grown more intense? Readers want to know, and the suspense of not knowing will carry them along for a while.

You can, of course, use more than two points of view. There can be three, four, five, as many as we have space for. But the problem is that control of the story becomes an issue. A few writers can handle it—Tom Clancy and Richard Condon come to mind—but things do tend to get complicated when we pile on the points of view. Differing points of view on the same theme or circumstances work best when there is some conflict. For example, two people talking about a recent death:

"He gave me my first job, I'll always be grateful."
"You never had him for a father, you wouldn't feel that way if you did."

Or coming upon the scene of a freeway crash:

She didn't want to stop, she couldn't stop, it was like the night after graduation when they raced to the beach house, and she saw the fireball of Billy's car catapult over the rail.

His adrenaline pumped as he slammed on the brakes and jumped from the bucket seat. His first on-road emergency, they'd told him it would be scary, but all he felt was exhiliration.

Or waiting for a phone call:

He fingered the change in his pocket, willing the caller to make contact. He wanted reassurance—and a strange measure of satisfaction—in hearing a voice, knowing there was a connection.

No, no no! God, no! Don't let the phone ring, she pleaded silently. They don't really have her, she stopped off at Miriam's yesterday, somebody forgot to call. What's twenty-four hours? Miriam'll be by later. . . .

Two points of view on the same subject, differing reactions, differing concerns. Within the same scene we could flip back and forth (sometimes using quick cuts or charged language as we examined in chapter four), and the conflict between the points of view would be highlighted. Note, too, that as the conflict occurs, the action (as in the freeway crash scene) or the suspense (as in the other two scenes) grows more intense.

Think in terms of intensity: The man wants the phone to ring, the woman doesn't. Now, let's carry the story further: The man vocalizes his wishes; the woman tells him he can't have the facts straight; the man points out (perhaps thinks about it first) that the woman tends to get hysterical in a crisis; the woman grows coldly angry, remembering other incidents when the man has treated her with disdain; the man remembers training he has received in coping with a kidnap situation, never thought it would happen to him, personally; the woman falls back on her version of reality, and she won't hear any other version.

And then the phone rings.

Conflict is sharper at the end than at the beginning, and that is how it should be. Whose viewpoint controls? It doesn't matter as long as tension keeps building.

Step by step, tauter and tauter. Then . . .

Someone blinks, and the story changes course.

ME, MYSELF AND I

One person, one point of view, right? Consider:

I watched them unload this sorry-looking catch of human futility, and I felt only disgust—not with these at-sea refugees, whose float from Haiti to anywhere civilized would never find a welcome—but with. . . .

Here's an observer and a commentator on the developing scene, a single point of view, one person. There's conflict (disgust, refugees caught attempting to smuggle themselves into the country), and as events unfold we'll probably have action because some of these people will not want to return to Haiti, and they might try to escape. If we zeroed in on one or two characters in particular, we could shift point of view. For example, we might be able to develop some suspense by showing that they are not what they seem to be—frightened political exiles—when they are really agents of the Haitian secret police, gathering information for later use. Who do they target, why, and what will happen? Suspense lingers.

But it's still one person, one point of view.

Now, try this: What if a character carries on a conversation with himself? An inner dialogue that never leaves the head! Almost like playing tennis alone, hitting the ball, then running to the other court to hit it back, then reversing and running. . . .

Single-handed tennis. Could it work?

It's interior monologue/stream of consciousness and we saw how it worked with dialogue in chapter five. Now we can apply it to a shifting point of view in the same way: one person, one mind, two points of view.

For example, take a look at James Joyce's *Ulysses*, in which the mind of Leopold Bloom flits to trousers and a loosened fly and the posting of advertisements any old place . . . and where then might such an advertisement be placed?

One part of his mind suggests the open fly.

The other part registers surprise, then says No, No!

The first part reluctantly agrees.

One person, *two* points of view! If Joyce had wished, he could have lengthened this so the conflict would expand, but even so, there is initial disagreement, and that should keep the reader's attention.

Two points of view within the same head should be judiciously used; it is not *that* common, nor should it be. Yet it can serve a good purpose. See, for example, *Any Woman's Blues* by Erica Jong (Harper & Row), in which the protagonist, Leila, has periodic conversations with "Sane Mind"—herself—when crises arise; the conversations, or points of view, are set off with italics and occur regularly, and they don't always agree with one another! We get a different side of the character's personality and get caught up in the struggle between the two points of view. This will provide a spur to action or suspense taking place outside the character's head, because the character's reaction shows the effect is strong enough to make her talk to—or argue—with herself.

The stronger the internal reaction, the more intense the external happenings; the greater the conflict inside the head, the more graphic the events outside the head.

- A person argues with himself over committing a murder. Doesn't the suspense of whether it will happen grow commensurately?
- A rape victim hears voices telling her not to report the crime. Don't her demeanor and interpersonal relationships grow more strident, more angry; isn't there more action?

Action and suspense can be enhanced through developed internal conflicts. The story moves forward, and characterizations are broadened. But *be careful!* Remember to:

- use them sparingly (because one character's internal conflicts can't carry a book entirely).
- limit each internal conversation to a few lines; don't run them on for a page or more.
- develop two *distinct* points of view.
- make sure the points of view are in conflict.
- keep the points of view tied to the surrounding action and/or suspense.

Because, above all else, we're trying to *build* our action and suspense. And to do that well we have to prepare a good foundation.

CHAPTER 9

SUBTLETY AND MISDIRECTION

A CAR ENGINE BREAKS the stillness of the night . . . the smell of seaweed intrudes on an afternoon chess game . . . an unopened letter slips behind couch cushions. . . .

These are what we might call "plot-hypers," in that they add an element of uncertainty and tension. They create a rise of anxiety by injecting an unexplained event or circumstance. What makes plot-hypers especially useful is the relative ease with which they can be used and the impact they can have on a story.

Think of Arthur Conan Doyle's *The Hound of the Baskervilles*, in which Sherlock Holmes discovers that on the crucial evening the watchdog did *not* bark, thereby offering the clue that ultimately solves the case. The plot-hyper is the dog's *not* barking, and its relevance, of course, is not explained until the end of the story.

Or consider "The Purloined Letter" by Edgar Allan Poe in which the letter thief, in front of witnesses, places an inoffensive letter alongside an important letter and a few moments later picks up the important letter and walks away. The police prefect knows the identity of the letter thief, holds a low opinion of him (because he is a poet), and is certain an efficient police search will uncover the stolen letter. Yet the letter thief foils the police by leaving the stolen document in plain sight, where he is sure no one will think to look. And it almost works. The plot-hyper here is in the police prefect's underestimation of the letter thief, and the plot-hyper's relevance blossoms when the letter cannot be found.

Note the subtlety and misdirection: Neither Conan Doyle nor Poe has hit the reader over the head to build suspense or develop action. One little fact, one simple assumption, and the story proceeds on a track that is much different from what we might expect. Conan Doyle relied on subtlety, Poe on misdirection (the reader *assumes* the stolen letter must be hidden away when, actually, it was right in plain sight all the time). Plot-hypers are the tools that make subtlety and misdirection possible. They create uncertainty that might—but doesn't have to— complicate things. They raise the tension level. What plot-hypers require is a sense of proportion that tries to keep the cat in the bag while opening the bag enough so the cat can breathe.

We speak of subtlety and misdirection because the story moves with veils and whisps and bare outlines, and there's no attempt to ring a bell or blow a whistle so the reader's attention can be lassoed like a runaway calf. What this type of writing requires is a careful assessment of how much or how little to offer the reader, keeping in mind that we don't want to be unfair, and we don't want to obfuscate beyond a reasonable point. It means we must come up with at least one plot-hyper, and we must plant the key somewhere in the text. It doesn't do much good if we expect the reader to deduce things from vague clues because, then, we've exchanged subtlety for unreasonable expectation. Go back to Conan Doyle and Poe—both planted their plot-hypers in the body of their stories, the subtleties and misdirection came, not from obfuscation or vagueness, but from knowledge of the way we tend to think. How many of us are lulled by the steadiness of routine? The same thing done the same way at the same time and in the same place. Would we wonder about sinister consequences if the routine broke down once or twice? Human nature, we'd call it, nothing works perfectly *every* time!

Of course, Sherlock Holmes wasn't quite so fooled.

How many of us go on a search and assume we must look behind something or inside something or under something or above something—that what we're searching for must be *hidden*, in the sense that it can't be picked out by the naked eye? Poe showed us that the best hiding place may well be somewhere in plain sight because human nature assumes this could never be a possibility. If we're searching for something, it must be *hidden!*

Why do we use subtlety and misdirection in the first place? And do they really enhance the way we build action and suspense? The answers lie in the simple equation that becomes an element of the partnership we develop with our readers: The longer we keep our readers guessing, the more attention they will pay to what they are reading. Subtlety and misdirection are tools to keep the reader guessing and reading. Simple as that.

See the difference:

The blackened mask had two slits for the eyes and a triangular hole where the nose would fit. Lips pierced by clawlike teeth were painted where the mouth would have been, and my mind screamed the question . . . would I be victim or victimizer this time?

or

"I didn't know you'd gone to acting school," she said.

He laughed. "My father's idea. I only lasted two months, and I was pretty bored." He pushed himself from the chair. "What about that pizza?"

Assume that both of these selections deal with the same suspenseful topic—a sinister mask and how it affects the person who is wearing it. The selections come from different directions, but they both seek to develop suspense. In the first selection, there's no attempt to hide the horrid implications; the mask is described, as are its possible effects. No subtlety here, no misdirection, only a straightforward depiction of a suspenseful event.

In the second selection, we have the subtlety, and we see it through the use of the plot-hyper. Note that the dialogue presents itself on two levels: as a simple conversation about attending acting school and *as a clue to what this might mean later.* It's the second level that concerns us, and we should ask ourselves what the conversation actually implies.

The answer is: What can a person learn at acting school?

Makeup techniques, characterization techniques. Two months of study would be enough to learn some of these techniques, and the results could have sinister consequences as the story moved along.

The plot-hyper is the character's attending acting school, but note that's all the information we're given. The next line of dialogue changes the subject and the focus. An alert reader would catch the plot-hyper and might discern its relevance, even though its full impact won't come until later in the story. But subtlety and misdirection make the plot-hyper work by:

- offering a thread of information.
- forcing the reader to deduce the relevance.
- not highlighting the information (making it seem a natural outgrowth of the conversation) but not burying it either — remember, no unreasonable obfuscation.

Suspense and action both can use subtlety and misdirection to give them depth and zip. Uncertainty is the lifeblood of suspense, and when we provide a bare clue about something sinister that's already happened, is happening or will happen, we can't help but heighten the uncertainty. The clue won't give the answer, we're only offering a whisp of something, but it does juice up the suspense.

Or with action sequences, things *happen*. Suppose a fact is misread or ignored (such as out-of-date blueprints that become the basis for a rescue during a construction fire). The subtlety or misdirection comes in avoiding overemphasis of the plot-hyper — the use of the old blueprints, for example — and keeping things simple. Mention the wrong blueprints in passing, or have the character unaware they have been superseded. Yet play fair with your readers, give them a chance to catch the subtlety or misdirection. But don't make it too easy!

A brief mention or two, a veiled reference, and you've done your job. Now it's the reader's turn.

HINTS AND SHADOWS

"You've got to have respect for your reader," said a former writing teacher of mine. I was to hear it many times. "Let the reader in on the story, don't push him away, don't assume he *shouldn't* know."

The first time I heard these words was when my teacher returned a mystery-suspense story I had written. I hadn't wanted to give the denouement away, so I had—at least to my own mind—craftily hidden the crucial facts. Unfortunately, it would have taken a professional treasure-hunter to find the key, because I had placed much more emphasis on hiding than on showing. In other words, my goal—which I wasn't aware of—had been to create a great hiding place rather than to develop a clue or a plot-hyper.

"It's an ends-means thing," my writing teacher said. "Your goal should not be to hide something, your goal should be to show it sensibly enough so a careful reader might pick it up or suspect that something isn't right. Maintain respect for your reader, it will come back to you a thousandfold."

Think of an iceberg, he went on, noting that Hemingway used this concept. Seventh-eighths is under water and hidden. But we know *something* is there because we can see the tip. When we write with subtlety and misdirection, that's the way we should think and develop a story line. "Hints and shadows," my teacher added, "they will carry the message that something is there, and then it's up to the reader's imagination to supply the bulky possibilities. For the moment you needn't go any further."

Hints and shadows are the product of writing with subtlety and misdirection. A woman faces a man she hates; does she shout her venom at him, or does she make a white-knuckled fist and speak politely?

A sailing yacht cruises the south Atlantic; do the occupants realize the long-range navigational gear is unreliable or do they laugh off a couple of celestial fixes that don't square with their dead-reckoning plot?

A man tends to stutter whenever uniformed policemen are

nearby, but is the connection explained or commented upon?
Hints and shadows.

What types of circumstances or events might offer possibilities? How about:

- physical habits (uncommented upon, of course)
- out-of-place remarks
- misplaced items
- weird physical reactions from inanimate objects
- unexplained absences
- unexpected presences

Any of these become hints or shadows that can affect the story line, and so long as they remain uncommented upon, or barely referred to (and ultimately have a strong impact on the story), they work their subtle influence on what happens. Each of them is a plot-hyper, yet none of them need rise up and slap the reader in the face: *"Hey! Look at me! I mean something to the story!"* The careful reader will catch the plot-hyper and wonder about its meaning and how it will affect the story without a lot of stage directions from the writer. That's the only reaction we want at this point. We want to keep the reader guessing and interested. We don't want to explain the significance of the plot-hyper; we want the reader's imagination to take over.

Take a look at how Herman Wouk handled a plot-hyper in *The Caine Mutiny* (Doubleday), his story of the growing paranoia of Philip Queeg, the captain of a U.S. Navy ship during World War II. For a while we get no inkling that Queeg is neurotic, except for a certain physical habit—a hint or shadow—that the author describes but never comments upon. The first time we come upon the physical habit is when Queeg is ready to relieve the departing captain, De Vriess, and take over the ship. They are sitting comfortably in the captain's cabin, drinking coffee:

> Queeg reached into his pocket. De Vriess, expecting him to pull out cigarettes, picked up a packet of matches. But Queeg brought out a couple of bright steel ball bearings the size of marbles and began rolling them absently be-

tween the thumb and fingers of his left hand.

At no time does the author comment on the significance of the steel balls, merely that they make an appearance, usually when Queeg is under some strain. What are we to make of this physical act? It borders on the bizarre, certainly, and that should tell us it isn't a habit without some importance to the story. Different, for example, from someone casually smoking a cigarette or absently stroking a beard. We should ask ourselves: Why would the author include this physical habit if he wasn't trying to make some point? The bizarre nature of the habit should light up our curiosity, and we should follow the habit's progress through the story.

The steel balls are a hint and shadow of Queeg's growing paranoia. They offer a clue that he is mentally ill, but the author wisely refrains from discussing this (until much later in the story), thus pushing the reader to wonder what the steel balls really mean. Uncertainty in the reader translates to suspense in the story, and that's one of the things Herman Wouk was trying to create.

The next time the steel balls appear is when Queeg meets his officers in the wardroom after he has relieved the command. He places a pack of cigarettes in front of him:

> He tore open the pack deliberately, lit a cigarette and took the two steel balls out of his pocket. Rubbing them softly back and forth in his fingers he began to speak.

Here, once again, the author doesn't try to explain the significance of the steel balls. They exist, they appear when Queeg feels a strain, and the reader is left to wonder how important they are to the story.

Note the subtlety *and* the misdirection in all of this: Queeg appears fit, mentally and physically, with only that one small, strange habit, which many readers wouldn't see as significant. It takes a careful reader to *understand*. Nothing's hidden, nothing unfair is done.

But the reader has to be paying attention.

Because hints and shadows don't trumpet their appearance
. . . or their disappearance.

FORESHADOWING

There are hints and there are HINTS. Those slight, subtle
whisps touched on above are garden-variety, lowercase hints,
small effects that move the story and may or may not signal
something momentous later on. They are important storytelling
tools, important plot-hypers, to be sure, but what they hint at
may or may not be crucial to the story's central theme. (Okay,
the steel balls *were* crucial in *The Caine Mutiny*, but they weren't
telling us that something specific would happen later, only that
something strange was happening *now*.)

But HINTS—uppercase variety—live and breathe with
story significance. These are the heavyweights, and when they
appear, the story will be bound to change substantially at some
point in the future. HINTS are always crucial to the story's central theme; they are saying that something big and challenging
will be happening later.

Both varieties—hints and HINTS—are plot-hypers, different in degree rather than kind; they both add something to the
story, and they both charge it with uncertainties. Yet one tends
to reflect the present, the other tends to promise that something
will happen later.

Now versus the *future*.

It is this latter type we also need to understand. HINTS,
rather than hints.

We know it as *foreshadowing*. Consider these:

- A character has an epileptic seizure. Will it occur again
  while he is climbing a precarious rock ledge?
- A character panics in the dark. Will she control the panic
  while imprisoned in a dark cave?
- A character is severely abused as a child. What kind of
  adult relationship will he have with spouse and family?

Each of these — epileptic seizure, panic in the dark, child abuse — are keys to how that character will react under similar or related circumstances at some point in the future. They *foreshadow* conduct and actions that will occur. They are HINTS about what will happen in the story.

Foreshadowing lays the groundwork; it provides an early sign. Note how the word has crept into our language: We *foreshadow* evil, his conduct is a *foreshadow* of things to come. It is a fine technique for developing suspense and extending action because it offers a *possibility* that will pick at the reader until the possibility either occurs or is discounted.

To develop suspense:

> A character shows unmistakable skill with code breaking but discounts it; later he is forced to use the skills during an emergency.

To extend action:

> A character was hailed as a genius sailboat racer when he was a boy, though one competitor thought he cheated; now, he is in an international yacht race. Will he cheat here, too?

The possibility is what's important, and that's what we foreshadow. Good writing would also dictate that we don't stand on a podium and shout, "Hey reader! Over here! Don't forget this! We're foreshadowing now."

We try to be subtle, to use misdirection, to establish some *style*. Take the two examples above:

> When he was thirteen, young Matt found double-crostic puzzles in the Sunday paper, and the next two years would never be the same. He loved the challenge of outwitting an adult mind that was so sure of superiority, and he would spend hours each week — forgetting his homework, house chores, even dinner sometimes — trying to make it come out.

and

Gareth liked to beat Blinky more than the others. Maybe because Blinky never offered anything but lukewarm congratulations after each win, and he felt he was entitled to more. Maybe because he caught Blinky inspecting his sails and rigging *after* several races, then speaking quietly to a member of the race committee. . . .

These are HINTS, especially if code breaking and yacht racing are major themes in the stories. Note the subtleties: Matt is not breaking a secret *code* at age thirteen, he's trying to solve a puzzle; Gareth is not accused of cheating, he's being checked on. These items foreshadow the later events sufficiently because, remember, all we want to provide is a HINT, not an answer.

And note something else. There's no reason why foreshadowing can't have conflict. In the second selection, Gareth and Blinky show conflict; in the first selection, Matt shows his disdain for the puzzle-maker. What does conflict do for foreshadowing? It keeps it dramatic (you knew that, didn't you?), it revs up the excitement. And while we don't want to wallow in the conflict (because this will call too much attention to the foreshadowing and kill the subtlety), a modest amount of conflict is fine and dandy.

Put all of this together, subtlety and HINTS and conflict, and see how James Dickey handles it in his novel *Deliverance* (Houghton Mifflin). It's the story of four city men who want to canoe a whitewater river in a remote section of Georgia before the wilderness will be lost to a dam and civilization. Before they leave, they have a meeting:

"There's one thing that bothers me," Drew said. "We don't really know what we're getting into. There's not one of us knows a damned thing about the woods, or about rivers."

They meet up with an old man deep in the woods, as they prepare to put their canoes in the water. He's strange looking with spotted hands that tremble.

"Man, I like the way you wear that hat," Bobby said to the old man.

The man took off the hat and looked at it carefully; there was nothing remarkable about it, but when it was on his head, it had the curious awkward-arrogant tilt that you find only in the country South. He put the hat back on the other side of his head with the same tilt.

"You don't know nothin'," he said to Bobby.

Here is foreshadowing. First, when Drew says they don't know anything about the forest or about rivers. That becomes apparent later on as they experience the horror and terror of the trip. There's conflict here in the sense that what they don't know (forests and rivers) is exactly what they will be facing, and the foreshadowing is pretty explicit. But then notice the conversation with the old man. Here's subtlety in foreshadowing because the author doesn't spell out that open, friendly Bobby courts disaster by shooting his mouth off. "Man, I like the way you wear that hat," may be a compliment to Bobby, but to the old man it's intrusive and insulting. And when the old man says "You don't know nothin'," he's showing his teeth, and the author is trying to portray—subtly—that Bobby will be victimized later on, as he assuredly is. The author is also saying that these travelers, Bobby especially, really don't know anything about the wilderness and the people who live there. This becomes apparent when they are set upon by mountain men who sexually abuse them and intend to kill them, and Bobby is their prime victim.

From the old man's conversation, we don't know exactly what will happen, but when he says "You don't know nothin'," a careful reader would sense danger and conflict . . .

And building drama. It's a plot-hyper, and it's subtle . . . of course.

REVERSING THE RULES

Human nature carries with it certain truisms: A kind person will be generally liked, a cruel person will be generally feared, an elderly person will be generally respected, a young person will be generally naive. These assumptions are based upon experiences through the millennia and the organic development and propensities of our moral and ethical codes. They become expectations that guide our lives, and we see them renewed again and again.

But good writing doesn't always follow the rules (here's another truism, but, somehow, it has a little more pizzazz), and when we consider our assumptions about human nature, we find it more interesting — and more exciting — to change things around. *Contrariness* is what some people call it, and it appears in a variety of settings (think of *contrary* investing, for example, where you avoid putting your money with the majority point of view). When people are "contrary," they are going against the established way of doing things, they "move against the flow," "march to their own drummer," "dissent from the norm." They may frustrate the majority when consensus is sought, but no one can debate the spark of excitement they create.

It works this way with writing, too. We lean on readers' expectations, as we discussed in chapter six. Then we flip them around so everything's changed. It's subtlety and misdirection at work. A reader *expects* something to be a certain way, but suddenly it's not. The misdirection is in the expectation, and the subtlety is in the surprise.

We reverse the rules:

- a handsome man who is cruel
- an evil character who loves children
- a saintly organization with rot underneath

If we hadn't reversed the rules, the handsome man would be kind and loving, the evil character would hate children, and the saintly organization would operate ethically from top to bottom. These are the conclusions our *expectations* would demand, but by reversing the rules we don't allow the reader to wallow in a rut of disinterest (if the reader *expects* things to be a certain way, pretty soon the subconscious is going to yawn and ask, "So what else is new?"). We keep the reader guessing, off balance, uncertain . . . and interested!

Consider these examples from literature:

- Jim, the runaway slave in Mark Twain's *The Adventures of Huckleberry Finn,* can barely read and write, but he has more innate wisdom than any other character.
- Mildred in W. Somerset Maugham's *Of Human Bondage* is beautiful and sexy and totally cruel and deceptive.
- Jay Gatsby in F. Scott Fitzgerald's *The Great Gatsby* is handsome, generous, debonaire, wealthy and a gangster.

Each of these authors reversed the rules on the characters, not allowing the reader's expectations to control who they were and what they did. Instead, the authors turned the characters into something different, giving them more substance and certainly making them more interesting.

But unexpected characterizations aren't the only way we reverse the rules. We can do it with setting:

A nunnery with a sisterly serial killer

We can do it with plotting:

A burglary ring that never seems to get it right, but succeeds in spite of itself

The point is that reversing the rules applies to most writing situations, and the story will generally be enhanced. Here's a good approach:

1. Understand the reader's expectations about a predominant aspect of your characters and situations. What's the norm, what's usual?

2. Think conflict. Develop characters and situations that conflict with one another such as the handsome man who is also cruel or the nunnery that has a serial killer.

3. Make sure the reversal plays an important part in the developing story. Don't do it for cosmetic reasons (the cruelty

of the handsome man must move the plot, for example).

4. Don't overdo the reversals. It isn't necessary to work it with every situation or character. Pick and choose where it will make the greatest impact and develop the most interesting situation or character.

Action and suspense stories live by an approach such as reversing the rules. As things happen and uncertainties grow, we must be able to keep the reader out of that rut of disinterest.

Presto-change-o!, we say, and what the reader expects is not what the reader gets.

CHAPTER 10

TIME AND PLACE

THERE USED TO BE A late-night television talk show called "Open End," hosted by David Suskind. The format was a roundtable discussion that attempted to probe a subject deeply. What made the show unusual was that it didn't have a cutoff time. It continued until the host decided things had been sufficiently explored, and then he signed off. In any given week, the show might run from an hour to three or four hours depending upon the extent of the discussion.

Hence the name "Open End." Content was more important than arbitrary time limits, and it was truly a noble experiment in a field where the clock is immutable. But the show also made people nervous because the element of time was downgraded. "It's too unstructured," came the comment, "too uncertain." Other criticism was levelled at the fact that David Suskind could become a programming czar because he controlled how much or how little of his show would go over the air. Some type of brake was essential.

What the critics were really saying was that a better show would result if content could be played against the limitations of time, that time constraints *force* a more cohesive product. The arguments on this point don't end, of course, but the thing to note is this: What time control and time limitations do for television programming they also can do for action and suspense writing. If a better story can blossom from working within rather than beyond the demands of hourly television time, why can't a better story be written in a time frame that is limited and narrow and precise?

In other words, why push time and its influence to a back burner? Ask yourself this: Does the passage of time have an effect on where my story is going? If so, then the elements of time must be beefed up. Just as the plot-hyper can add to subtlety and misdirection (as we saw in the previous chapter), the elements of time can create groundwork to support action and suspense. Stories play *against* time, creating conflict and a springboard for things to happen and for a rising uncertainty.

But time isn't alone in doing this, there's also setting to consider. The *place* where something happens can be just as important as time in creating limits and controlling events. We know, for example, that mountain climbing can be a dangerous activity, and it doesn't require a leap of inductive reasoning to see that a story set on the slopes of a forbidding mountain and involving a climbing party has the essentials for action and suspense. The place where the story occurs will control what happens and how it happens.

We wouldn't start the climbers off on their quest and then shift story focus to a sailing adventure in the Caribbean. This would confuse the reader who had become comfortable with the mountain climbing setting and must now readjust to something new . . . while wondering what will eventually happen with that mountain climbing sketch. Readers don't forget story setting, especially where the writer has painted a dramatic scene, and if the story focus shifts, there's bound to be some grumbling, if not outright resentment: *I'm confused! Is this writer playing games with me?. . .*

Slam! . . . *Thunk!* . . . "Don't bother reading this book. It's not worth your time."

So we must think of the limits that a certain setting puts upon us (just as we must remember the ongoing partnership we have with our readers), and we must be prepared to stay within those limits. As the criticism of David Suskind's show demonstrated, our failure to restrict ourselves with time and place will cause uncertainty in our audience — not about whether the characters will prevail but where the writer is going with the story line. It is an uncertainty based upon a budding lack of faith, a feeling that the writer is:

- playing unfair with the reader.
- unclear about story direction.

It would take a major rehabilitation for this writer to restore this reader's staunch faith.

When we combine setting or place with time, we have a secure groundwork for our story. Not only does the place where the story occurs have limits, but the time within which the story develops also provides limits. Now we have a concreteness of story line against which we can create action and suspense. We have it double-layered, in effect.

Consider our mountain-climbing sketch:

- If the climbers took enough supplies for only five days, both the action of the dangerous climb and the suspense of whether they make it to the top keep the story focused and limited.
- If the question of supplies never comes up, the action might still be exciting, the suspense might still be riveting (because we still don't know if they'll make it), but there's no time element to work against. And something is definitely lost.

Isn't it?

THE LOGIC OF SETTING

There's an exercise I do with my writing students in order to develop their appreciation for the nuances of setting. The idea that the *place* where the story occurs influences conflict and the degree of action and suspense is hard to fathom for those who see character and plot as main story sparks. "What's so exciting about setting?" I'm asked. "Most stories can be set anywhere."

Wrong! And to prove it I ask the students to imagine their

stories produced for the stage. "Think theater," I urge them. "Imagine a stage and a set and your characters and plot coming alive. You must be concerned with limits," I say, "you must take advantage of certain lighting, backdrops, entrances and exits; you must work to give your set a personality.

"You must use your set the way a museum showcases a work of art.

"To enhance the overall product.

"You must not waste your setting!"

Consider: a darkened alley, a courtroom, a jail cell. On stage, these settings provide something special for the story — they mean *conflict*. Each of them offers the intuitive message: You step in here, you've got conflict (and note this is *before* there is a word of dialogue or any stage business). If the story is action or suspense-related, such settings can only drive up the story temperature.

So, I have students write their opening scene as if it is a stage play, and I urge them to pay close attention to how they are using their settings. "Settings should have personalities," I remind them. "They are *not* inert backboards for the story line to play against."

And then they begin to get it.

There is logic in settings. We have learned that consistency between a setting and the story line is essential if the reader is not to be confused. For example, a gritty mystery would not fare well if it was set amidst a romantic comedy; and a horror-suspense story would have problems if it was set in the unfolding of a miracle. We could inject conflict, action and suspense in large doses, but with an inept setting, the story credibility would vanish.

So we must think *logically*, and this means we must look to setting or place as an enhancer of the story line; it must help to move things along. Put another way: Once armed with how we want our story to proceed and knowing our characters, we should be able to pick out a setting that will aid development of the story line.

Suppose you're Agatha Christie, and you've come upon the old nursery rhyme about "Ten Little Indian Boys" and you see it as a perfect vehicle for a murder mystery. With each verse one of the little Indian boys disappears, and you see this mirroring the serial deaths of the characters. You even have a title, *And Then There Were None* (Dodd, Mead), but where do you set this story so the setting will help things along?

Here comes the logic of setting. We have multiple deaths, a lot of things going on and a large cast of characters. The first thing to realize is that a limit of some sort must be employed. A geographic limit, more than anything else, because these characters and the murders must be contained so events don't get confusing. Christie decided to make all the characters guests in a large country house, so now we have the "place" developed, and there are limits. People aren't moving all over the landscape, and the country house, itself, offers a forum for conflict because the characters constantly run into one another, discuss the growing list of murders and sometimes accuse one another. Action and suspense are enhanced, too, because the limited setting forces things to happen right under the readers' — and the characters' — noses.

But there's still one loose end. Though the characters play out their roles around the country house, there's nothing to prevent them from escaping the madness of the serial murders and rushing away from the house . . . except that the story takes place on an island, and *there is no escape*. This is the genius of Agatha Christie; she forces her characters to remain present, and both the action (the characters rushing about seeking to discern the murderer) and the suspense (who will be murdered next, who is the murderer?) are enhanced by this fact. With a story line like this, could the tale be set anywhere else but on an island? Wouldn't it have been less effective otherwise?

The logic of setting.

There are many examples in literature of this technique, and Agatha Christie, herself, used it a number of times. In *Murder on the Orient Express* (Dodd, Mead), she had her characters confined to the onrushing train while her detective, Hercule Poirot, slowly pieced the solution together. Once again setting enhanced the story line by limiting the geography and bunching the action and suspense together. The more acute the connection, the more effective the result.

Or see John Godey's *The Taking of Pelham One, Two, Three* (Putnam) where an entire subway train was commandeered and held hostage. Once again the geography, *the place*, is limited, and so the writer can build up the action and the suspense. The hijacking of the subway train is conflict-laden, to be sure, and as the menace of the hijackers becomes more pronounced, the action (especially by the rescuers) and the suspense (will the trapped passengers get free?) become vivid. There is logic here, too. Why not a subway train if one has a beef with the city and seeks major amounts of money and doesn't care if lives are lost? This setting enhances the story because an uncontrolled subway train is like a rogue elephant—capable of turning on those it once followed.

When we think of setting—or place—we must see it primarily in terms of how it can limit or control the story line. We must use it as a basis for building action and suspense because it will enhance them and provide an arena where conflict can flourish. Whether the setting is a ship or an office building or a cave or a sporting event (this list is *not* exclusive), understand what the geographic limits are and that they work well when they have a logical tie to the story line.

THE CRUNCH OF TIME LIMITS

You have twenty-four hours to find the murderer and save yourself from certain arrest.

How many stories have been based upon this simple formula? A character is in jeopardy, and the author provides a possible escape . . . *but* the character must take advantage of the escape within a set, limited time. Failure means disaster.

We have enough water for only two more days.

The jeopardy is present (once the water runs out, people die), but escape is difficult, especially where the characters are adrift on an ocean or lost in a desert or forest. More than anything else, chance could play a part here, if there is to be escape (a wind shift, a rescue plane, a familiar landmark). But the time limit—two days—is the foundation that everything else plays against. Failure, again, means disaster.

Setting time limits like these offers a perfect scenario for conflict, and most writers sense that intuitively. Certain questions are implied:

- Is there someone or something we are *against*?
- Does failing to meet the time limit put us in danger?
- In whose interests does the time limit work?

Answer these questions and the conflict or conflicts in the story should be readily apparent:

In three days a man's former wife is to be remarried and his young son wants to live with his mother; the man discovers the husband-to-be had been accused of murdering his own son but had never gone to trial; the former wife will hear no criticism of her husband-to-be.

Is there someone or something we are against? The husband-to-be, of course, and the remarriage.

Does failing to meet the three-day time limit put us in danger? Not us, perhaps, but certainly the young son.

Against whose interests does the time limit work? The son's.

Do we have conflict? You bet we do.

Time limits snare the reader into rooting for or against the protagonist. The time limit acts as a parameter for the story, a wall that forces the action to take place within a confined space. Time limits are similiar to the boards in a hockey game, the out-of-bounds lines in football and basketball, the gates in a slalom ski race. They control the pace and the direction of the action, and they force suspense to build because they are immutable. The passing of time makes the chances of success less and less certain, as the options run out until the time limit expires and we know what the outcome is.

We've got to find her before the police do; it's the only thing that can save us.

Here's another variation: no precise time set forth, only a circumstance. We don't know exactly when, but we do know what we have to do — find the woman.

Is there someone or something we are against? The police.

Does failing to meet the time limit (read, find the woman) put us in danger? Absolutely.

In whose interests does the time limit (finding the woman) work? Ours.

Is there conflict? What a question!

Take a look at the way Gerald Green handled time limits in *The Hostage Heart* (Playboy Press), the story of a wealthy man undergoing open-heart surgery. While the doctors are in the operating room, preparing to operate, a group of revolutionaries burst in, announcing they want ten million dollars and that they have their men stationed throughout the hospital. The doctors are directed to continue the operation while the money is collected, and the revolutionaries warn they are holding the patient and his heart hostage. They give the hospital authorities and the police two hours to get the money (until five minutes past noon), or they will kill the patient and shoot the doctors.

At one point, negotiations break down, and Trask, the leader, pulls the heart-lung machine plug.

"He has four minutes to live," Trask said . . . "or he might survive as a vegetable."

A few lines later there is agreement on terms, and Trask turns to the head doctor:

"How much time is left, Dr. Lake?"
"A minute, maybe a minute and a half."

And they start the machine up again, and the patient barely survives. The operation is almost over.

Lake looked at the wall clock: 11:55. He stepped back from the table and asked Flor to wipe his forehead. He wondered how long he could hold his people together.

Here are two separate applications of the time-limit crunch. When the wall plug is pulled, we find the patient will have only four minutes of pure life before deterioration sets in. The negotiations continue even as the seconds tick away, and when we're down to a minute and a half, things go back on track. Can't we imagine that panicky operating room and the helpless patient as the time limit draws ever nearer? The suspense grows excruciating. Will they agree on matters, will the patient survive, will everyone be safe?

The second time-limit crunch involves whether the money will arrive within the two-hour deadline. As the book moves along, the author sprinkles data about that two-hour time limit. And now just ten minutes before the limit, the head doctor isn't sure he can hold his people together, *and still the money hasn't arrived!*

The author plays his time-limit scenario like a virtuoso, keeping us aware of the time every few pages and stretching the suspense to the end. He keeps us guessing, and by doing that he has made that time-limit crunch almost audible. For example:

> The bridge'll blow in six minutes, we can't make it. Hurry!
> I'm scared, Bobby. . . .

And the reader will be, too.

INCIDENTS AND ANECDOTES

A common way to inject drama into a story is to create an incident or portray an anecdote, to provide a happening that will catch the reader's imagination. *Tell me a story* is another way of saying the same thing. We do not write *at* the reader.

The reader becomes part of the story and our omnipresent partner.

In a limited sense, we can use incidents and anecdotes to enhance the concept of "place," the setting in our stories. And the benefit is that the action and suspense will be enhanced as well.

But first, what are incidents? What are anecdotes?

For our purposes, an incident is nothing more than a happening, an event, a development. It could be a sudden meeting, a storm, a baby's cry, a noise in the night, anything, in fact, that can be billed as "a happening." It changes story pace and provides an opportunity to spur action and suspense:

> The barn seemed darker, mustier than she remembered . . . oh well, grab the pony's halter, and she'd be outside in a moment, and those two kids better not have run off . . . What was that in the shadows? It-it was moving . . . she heard raspy breathing. . . .

Here's an incident framed against an unsettling "place"—the dark and musty barn. Note there is already some tension in the scene by virtue of the barn's description, but now we add an incident—something in the shadows that moves and has raspy breathing—and the scene becomes more vibrant. The incident propels the action and the suspense already there and pushes them further. The reader should be hanging on every word.

The key is to think of setting, not simply as physical description, but as an expandable form of tension-building. Use an incident to *add* to the tension already there. Think imaginatively:

- *Action*: A balloon race *and* there is a tear in the balloon cuff. . . .
- *Suspense*: Parents wait anxiously for a teenager's telephone call *and* there is an electrical blackout. . . .

In both cases the incident (the balloon tear, the blackout) serves to heighten the tension and to give more substance to the underlying uncertainties of the setting. A balloon is not the safest of vehicles, and anxious parents do not project a calm atmosphere. There's tension in both of these settings, and it's expanded when the incidents occur.

The benefit? More vibrant action and suspense—and a turned-on reader.

It works the same way with anecdotes, which are stories within stories, vignettes that highlight something for a limited purpose. These, also, will add dimension to the story's sense of "place." An anecdote serves to inject drama into the story by offering a little tale with which the reader can identify. See how it works:

> As he walked by the shadowy old house, he recalled the day when poor Mr. Newsome came out on the second-floor balcony and shouted to the heavens: "Thank you, Lord, for this blessing! She is alive!" No one ever figured what he was talking about, and a month later the old man died.

The anecdote certainly will perk up the reader's attention, and if we're starting with a suspenseful setting—the shadowy old house—it will spur it even higher. An anecdote can come through narration or through dialogue, but it must inject drama into the story. It wouldn't do much good, for instance, to offer an anecdote about a recent sporting event when we're writing about returning to a home left twenty years before in disgrace. But if we supply an anecdote about feeling the sense of "home" over a recent Christmas dinner with friends, then it has relevance to the underlying story, and it can be used to buttress the action and suspense.

Here, again, let's think imaginatively:

- *Action*: A gangland confrontation, *and* one character relates a recent harsh beating of an informer, in detail.
- *Suspense*: A character is to meet and pay off a blackmailer, *and* he recalls how a close friend had been severely injured doing the same thing.

The sense of place—where the confrontation or payoff occurs, and what will happen there—is suspenseful, and when we add the anecdote, we push everything up a notch or so. It isn't enough that some thugs are menacing one another; one of them has to give a graphic depiction of what could happen if violence breaks out. It isn't enough that a blackmailing victim has to worry about paying off and whether he will continue to be bothered; he must compare his possible fate with what happened to a friend.

When we add some physical description (a movie back lot, a dark and lonely highway pull-off), we have the sense of place adequately portrayed, and the anecdotes expand the suspense already generated. Remember, the anecdote must tie in to the underlying setting or "place"; it must relate to it and hype the tension. The anecdote must say to the reader, "You think it's been exciting up to now? Take a look at this little story, then see where you are."

Excitement on a grand scale.

ANYTIME BUT THE PRESENT

Most of us have been exposed to Mark Twain, and the fact he wrote a century ago hasn't dimmed our pleasure. His humor and his poignant characterizations are etched in literary lore, and we see him as clearly today as our grandparents did. While Mark Twain is celebrated for his stories of life on the Mississippi, he also had an abiding interest in the way people lived many centuries earlier. In particular, he enjoyed the Arthurian legends, life at the Roundtable and in feudal England. He decided to write a book about all this, but being Mark Twain, he couldn't — or wouldn't — do it in the customary romantic, heroic, chivalric fashion.

Instead, he pictured himself as a knight: "No pockets in armor, can't scratch, cold in the head — can't blow — can't get at handkerchief, can't use iron sleeve, make disagreeable clatter when I enter church. . . ." The result was *A Connecticut Yankee in King Arthur's Court*, a sometimes gentle, sometimes savage burlesque of life in sixth-century England. What gave the story its oomph was the fact that Twain could twist facts and circumstances into bizarre shapes and still retain his story line. For example, he has the five hundred knights of the Roundtable ride to the rescue of King Arthur, not on mounted steeds, but on bicycles. At another point he has his nineteenth-century interloper introduce the game of baseball, and before long King Arthur's court has divided into teams and begun playing, while still in their armor.

In terms of action and suspense, the book fares modestly, but it illustrates a strategy that can benefit us all. Because he was dealing with history (even his own skewered brand of history), Mark Twain felt liberated to massage the story line in bold ways. He wasn't bound by the limits of the present where we simply *know* how certain things are supposed to be (think how our government runs, or doesn't run; it would be difficult to burlesque it as flagrantly as Twain did with King Arthur and the Roundtable because we'd have to deny certain truths, and that would cause the story to cave in). The great advantage of setting a story somewhere in history is that no one can be absolutely certain what actually happened. We may know facts and we may know perspectives, but there's a wide area that yearns for the writer's imaginative skill.

And here is where action and suspense can blossom. We can use the special effects that history offers to build up our story line, to heighten our conflict and make that reader taste each word!

Look at Mark Twain. He manipulated a legend to blast certain inviolable myths (such as the magic of Merlin, which becomes a con man's trickery, or the staunch intelligence of King Arthur, which becomes questionable when he daydreams about invading Gaul while injustices flare about him). Turning mythical characters into imperfect humans allows him to create strong conflict (because imperfections mean someone will not be happy), and this will lead to more exciting action and suspense.

Consider:

- A story set right after the Civil War. Can we not recreate war battles that scar survivors so they act out nightmares and dangerous confrontations? Can we not depict these nightmares and confrontations? Can we not embellish history?
- A story set in one of the first North Pole explorations. Can we not develop survival conflicts—both personal and

against nature — without sticking to the letter of the facts? We can embellish what it was like, yet retain the essence of the true tale.

How does history allow us to do this, when the present circumscribes us so much more? With history we have the parameters of the story in place, so we can use them as a jump-off place. Setting a story in the present means we have to pay much closer attention to actual truth because the audience is acutely aware of its limitations. We simply can't embellish the present the way we can the past, and the result is that the *time* of our story can provide a push to the action and suspense we want to portray. In effect, history offers a basket of special effects that can add vividness to our story. We saw how this works in chapter one where we discussed raising emotional levels. We enlarged on it in chapter four where we "left 'em hanging" through scene cuts and using strong verbs and charged language. Time gives us a springboard; these techniques allow us to soar.

The same principles apply to a story set in the future. Here again, we don't really know the truth of events, we can only suppose or project (with history we know facts and perspectives, but if none of us lived during the period in question, where's our level of truth?). Even more than history, perhaps, the future allows us to manipulate special effects and rev up action and suspense. *Time* allows us to do pretty much what we wish *because no one knows what will happen between now and the future or what will happen in* the future! Good science fiction writers apply the truths of science as we now know them, and they create their worlds as outgrowths of the world as we now know it, but otherwise we have no parameters whatsoever, only projections, and thus the field for special effects is wide open.

Consider:

- The twenty-second century, and an evil presence seeks uniform mind control. Are we bound by human ethics standards, by current legal or political standards? Don't action and suspense explode with this scenario?
- The twenty-first century, and there's been a breakdown

in the U.S. economic structure, and a severe depression has occurred. Conflict leading to strong action and suspense flow naturally from here.

These "what if . . ." situations give the writer's imagination free rein, and there isn't much doubt the substance and the level of action and suspense will grow and grow. Think of using history and the future as settings where the truths are few and the opportunities unlimited. Think of these as *time periods* with special effects that can paint a story brighter and develop characters sharper because the straps of contemporary truth have been loosened.

And a new reality beckons.

CHAPTER 11
_____

IT'S IN THE PACING

ONE OF MY SERIOUS pleasures is the science and art of horse racing, and I spend worthwhile hours feeding my interest. In many ways a classic horse race is a metaphor for the way we conduct our lives; the horses are judged for value by weight or age or prior experience (like humans). Some prefer to stay at the rear, others rush to the front, still others are content to settle in the middle of the pack and await a chance to move up. And a select few have the talent to make several moves in the course of the race. What strikes me (here's the science part) is the rational approach each trainer takes to the organized chaos of half-ton beasts pounding down a prepared track, separated by a knife-edge from disaster. "Make your move along the far turn," the trainer might tell the jockey. "Stay near the lead for the first mile." "Save ground around the first turn." Rational advice, all of it, and in its way instructive beyond the racetrack. What, after all, are the trainers *really* telling their jockeys?

Plan your race. Okay, that's like working out a story. None of us would dream of beginning without some idea of where we were going and how we would get there.

Understand your horse has limited strength and endurance. No horse, no story can stay on high hum permanently. There must be times to throttle back, to ease things in order to build to a new rush. If we — jockey and writer — don't do this, both horse and story will suffer from burnout — guaranteed.

Pace your race. Don't try to win immediately; save your horse for the right moment, maintain control. Ah, once more we're staring at the demands of writing a story. Just as a good jockey maintains a sense of pace, a good writer will understand that a story must have steady, in-the-middle-of-the-pack time, quick-paced time and a rush-for-the-finish-line time. The good writer controls pace in the same way the good jockey does, by keeping something in reserve until the appropriate moment, by recognizing there will be slow moments and not panicking because of them, by staying patient and finish-line oriented.

"Get to the middle of the track for the stretch run," the trainer might tell the jockey.

"Keep things clear and unambiguous," the good writer will say. "Make that ending certain and climactic!"

Here, then, is the happy result from a good sense of pace: a race that is won, a story that ends clearly, on an upbeat and with a reader who stayed along for the ride, page after page.

The key to good pacing is to recognize that there are moments of acceleration *and* deceleration in every horse race . . . and in every story. The good jockey and the good writer know when these moments should occur and will plan for them. The result may not be victory or literary kudos, but there will certainly be respect for the jockey/author's skill and understanding that any horse race or any story demands much more than pointing the horse down the track or punching up a programmed computer screen and shouting "Go!"

I don't want to belabor the racetrack analogy, but let me add this: If you've ever seen slow-motion footage of running thoroughbreds and their intense-faced jockeys in rainbow-hued silks, you'll understand the art and grace that are inherent in the sport . . . in the same way that we appreciate the art and grace that blossom in a paragraph by John Updike or a line by Annie Dillard. A good sense of pace is part of the artistic process—just as it is part of the rational, scientific process—because it increases our pleasure and satisfaction.

A sense of pace is crucial because the reader will be turned off if there is no variety in story sequences. We've already seen what it's like if action scene follows action scene, suspense scene follows suspense scene, without a break or a slowdown so the reader—and the story—can take a collective breath. Pretty soon the abnormal becomes normal, and the reader, seeking variation, will lose interest.

Suppose, for example, we're writing a story that involves a major chase. Would each chapter contain a hair-raising confrontation between chaser and chasee, with the chasee barely escaping to live another day and occupy another chapter? Would chaser and chasee face danger, not necessarily from one another but from the elements or third parties or from themselves, every chapter?

Of course not. It would be too much, and the story would ultimately lose its vibrance. A better way to deal with the chase is to:

- have a confrontation between chaser and chasee early, have the chase proceed sedately for a while, *then* have another confrontation near the end.
- have chaser ponder the worth of the chase.
- have chasee ponder the worth of continuing to run.
- have a third party deflect chaser's attention from the chase.
- have a trusted friend almost betray chasee.

We could add to this list, of course, but the point is there isn't all action or all suspense, scene after scene, chapter after chapter. There are breaks in the action (the times when chaser and chasee ponder their effort, for instance), there's slowdown time (third party deflecting chaser), there's subplot time (chasee's *near* betrayal), and there's always the promise of further action and suspense (as long as the chase continues).

Here is the essence of pacing—some speed-up time, some slowdown time—not too much of either, but enough so the reader hangs on for the ride, interested, excited, and wondering what will happen next.

LET'S TAKE A BREATHER

Slowing down the pace is an important part of developing an overall story strategy. *Every* story must have its slow-pacing time, just as every story — especially stories with action and suspense — must have conflict and tension. When we put together a story plan, slow-pacing times must be carefully inserted and must blend with other scenes where action and suspense are highlighted. Note this, too: It's unlikely there will be only one slow-paced time in any book-length manuscript. The chances are there will be several, and they must be carefully placed throughout the entire story for maximum effect.

One good technique for creating slow-paced time is the flashback, where characters are removed from the story present and reappear at some earlier time in their lives.

> The soft mist off the lake reminded him of the fishing excursions Uncle Ed and he would take when he was so young. Everything seemed magical. "How many fish you want to catch today, boy?" Uncle Ed would murmur.

And we would be off exploring the boy's relationship with his uncle and the manner of his growing up. It would be a characterization study, and obviously the action and suspense would be minimized. Now, a flashback such as this should be shrewdly placed so it can contrast with action and suspense scenes yet offer something new for the reader, too. So, the story plan must be considered, and this flashback must *fit* in the sense that the story line remains uninterrupted and consistent. It does little good to insert a flashback that adds nothing to story progression and is, somehow, inappropriate. The flashback must be woven into the fabric of the story and tell us something more about the characters, the circumstances of the story, and the ultimate story resolution.

Take the flashback above. The protagonist might have been exploring the shoreline of the lake for a clue to a grisly murder when he spied the mist. The search for the clue would be suspenseful, possibly because he had just escaped from a nearly fatal roadside accident (which would be *action* oriented). One action scene plus one suspense scene might be enough so it becomes time to slow the pace down, and that's where the flashback comes in. We're transported elsewhere, away from the high tension that followed from one scene to the next, to a time and a place where tension is scaled back. Then, after a bit of time with the flashback, we can return to the action and suspense until it's time to scale things back again.

In the meantime, as the protagonist ponders his early fishing trips, we begin to understand him better and see, perhaps, why he might be involved in a murder mystery. It becomes a matter of character and characterization.

But flashbacks can do more than this. They can add an element to the plot, a missing detail, some hidden motivation, perhaps even a solution to the mystery. And they can do this even as they slow things down: *I recall that . . . Yet when I was sixteen, my mother decided I needed. . . .*

And equally as important, slow-paced flashbacks don't have to run on for pages. They can be a paragraph, even one line, as long as they contrast with an action or suspense sequence immediately before and contribute, in some way, to story movement. The point is this: Flashbacks, because they deal with the past, even if that past is brought up to the present, don't ring with the immediacy of the contemporary story; they remain something out of the past, and their natural inclination is to slow things down because they do not offer that sense of immediacy. Flashbacks are to tension-filled moments as an old sweater is to current fashion: useful and comfortable, a pleasure to lounge in but with limited purpose.

It works the same way with scene changes, which, incidently, can also be flashbacks. They cut away from the action, sometimes for only a half page or so, but long enough so there can be a change of pace. (In chapters two and four we used quick scene cuts to highlight shifts in point of view and build-up of conflict. Now we see they can be used to control pacing, as well.) It might be a sedate narrative passage following a scene of high drama and heavy action . . . or a scene of comfortable dialogue following a suspense-filled narrative . . . or even a scene of growing tension in a new subplot following a scene of lessening tension in an older subplot. The point is that the scene change can cause a variation in the level of action and suspense and generate a continuing interest in what's happening. Without the change of pace, the reader will grow weary and turn away.

See how an accomplished writer handles it: In Michael Crichton's *Jurassic Park* (Knopf), an island off Costa Rica has been turned into a tourist park where, through advanced scientific cloning and breeding procedures, a colony of prehistoric dinosaurs and other extinct animals has been developed. However, as a group of eminent scientists tour the park prior to its official opening, something goes wrong, and the prehistoric creatures break out of their enclosures and begin hunting humans. One of the characters is Malcolm, a mathematician-philosopher, who has been dubious about the project from the beginning. Periodically, the author will have Malcolm explain to the others certain scientific truisms that form the basis for his underlying skepticism.

When do Malcolm and his explanations occur?

You guessed it. Right after highly charged action and/or suspense. Here's Malcolm following a scene where frantic efforts to radio an island supply boat for help have finally paid off. Some characters are wringing their hands about the safety of the world should these prehistoric creatures make it to the mainland. Malcolm scoffs at their egomania.

> "Let me tell you about our planet," he said. "Our planet is four and a half billion years old. There has been life on this planet for nearly that long. Three point eight billion years. . . ."

Malcolm's discourse carries almost a page, and the scene, itself, only runs two and a half pages. But the slowdown and the more sedate pace are palpable, especially when prior scenes flip from one dangerous, threatened locale to the next, and each one depicts characters in crisis. Then it's on to Malcolm who explains . . . and explains. . . .

And we have a breather before the action and suspense pick up again.

CRISIS, CRISIS!

A mountain climber hangs by a thin, frayed line above a rocky canyon.

A woman is on her way to meet the mother who gave her up for adoption when suddenly she can't breathe.

A man and woman discover their major assets have been lost because their investment advisor made risky purchases.

The common thread here is crisis. *Crisis!* The characters are faced with events for which they didn't plan and that can destroy or severely damage them. The characters face crises, and the manner in which they overcome the crises gives us the measure of the writer. Do the characters do it with grace and aplomb, do they do it with high intellect or with cleverness, or do they do it haltingly, unevenly, clumsily? The writer will be judged by the ability to resolve these circumstances for the characters.

All stories need crises; crises are where tension erupts, where conflict abounds (note in the three examples above, the conflict can be between individuals as well as between the individual and the environment). Crises are where the tautness comes in stories, and where a sense of pacing must not be overlooked. But no story can work with one crisis feeding directly into the next, leaving little room for breathers and more sedate scenes. Crisis after crisis after crisis may seem appropriate because we want to keep the reader excited and tuned in, but after a while if the crises are continuous, their urgency ceases because a sense of normality creeps in. A crisis on page 10 followed by other crises become customary events by page 120 (that is, *you* may think they're new crises, but the reader doesn't see them that way any longer).

A yawn, a sigh, and the reader wonders what might be on television.

So we do ourselves and our readers a favor by managing our crises so they don't run up against one another, so they are spaced out (I don't mean in the hallucinogenic sense), so they are "sprinkled" through the story. The goal is to build up to the crises, then play each one out, then drift off for a while until it's time to build to a new crisis. There's no rule about the number of crises a story should have, all writers must feel these things for themselves, but we can say this: A crisis is only useful when it forces characters to confront weaknesses or uncertainties because then we're doing what most great writers advise—we're moving the story forward and/or we're developing character. Either way we're changing the story landscape, and that's what readers are looking for.

Why? Because there's challenge and interest in each new step the story takes. Readers want the unexpected, they want to be entertained, and something new gives them what they want. If we want to maintain our reader-writer partnership and work *with* our readers, this is what we must offer.

A crisis is that crucial moment when circumstances or people change, usually without warning. Suppose, for example, we're writing a story of deception and intrigue among the members of a large, well-to-do family. The family leader is a ninety-year-old woman who is near death, but no one is willing to take family control because her presence remains intimidating. The relatives scheme surreptitiously, hoping to grab some family assets before facing the uncertainty of her will. Questions come right at us: Will someone try to kill the old woman? Which family members are in conflict? Who is doing the scheming and what do they want?

These questions form the basis for one or more crises:

- *Will someone try to kill the old woman?* An attempt is made (the crisis) and suddenly the relatives are scared and suspicious of one another.
- *Which family members are in conflict?* Two relatives have a fistfight over a piece of sculpture (the crisis) and an air of mutual antagonism follows.
- *Who is doing the scheming, what do they want?* A relative admits she has filed court papers to have the old woman declared incompetent (the crisis) and to have herself appointed guardian.

Each crisis, then, becomes a turning point in the story where attitudes and the reader's perceptions will change. Each crisis should create as many questions as it answers, so the reader continues to be uncertain about where things will end. But note this: All these crises can develop in the same story, and they will prove effective to maintain conflict *providing we space them out, so they don't follow one on top of the other.*

That's the key. Pacing, again. Crises are like breathers in that they need to be inserted with a good eye on the way the story is being paced. Is the story meandering or the sense of conflict blunted? Perhaps it's time to add a crisis. Our good eye must stay focused on the overall flow of events, on how each story segment fits with other story segments so there's no unnatural bulge in the story line. Crises, like breathers, change circumstances, events and perceptions, and for this reason they must be sprinkled. A run of sedate writing should be followed by a crisis (just as a couple of high-powered scenes should be followed by some sedate writing), so the reader can never grow too comfortable.

THE NARRATIVE WAY

Suppose a story begins this way:

> The sporting men of Mulligan's were an exceedingly knowing lot; in fact they had obtained the name amongst their neighbors of being a little bit too knowing. They had "taken down" the adjoining town in a variety of ways. They were always winning maiden plates with horses which were shrewdly suspected to be old and well-tried performers in disguise.

The narrative continues for another page and a half before the first line of dialogue creeps in, and then we're off on a romp involving a sting that goes wrong and a seemingly innocent priest who ends up with most of the money. The story is "The Downfall of Mulligan's" by Banjo Paterson, and the action centers on the poker table and the racetrack. It is not a long story, but it shows how narrative can dominate pacing and retain the reader's interest.

Up to now we've been examining the need for *change* of pace, intermixing breathers and crises so our readers remain—figuratively and literally, we hope—on the edge of their seats. We don't want to drone on, and we don't want to be overbearing, so we change speeds and try to keep the excitement high.

But Banjo Paterson's story shows us there are times when we don't have to change the pace, when the underlying action builds steadily, when anecdotes and character development carry things along without alternating between crises and breathers. The story is 90 to 95 percent narrative (there are but ten separate dialogue passages in all); the only crisis comes at the end when the sporting men of Mulligan's lose their money and find they have been outschemed. There are no breathers. The only character given serious dimension is the priest (no other character is provided a name or a calling) and everything builds from a slow beginning to that ultimate crisis and climax.

Here, then, is *narrative pacing*, that is, pacing without dialogue shifts or quick scene cuts or sharp point-of-view changes. It wouldn't work well over the length of a book because its unbroken rhythm would eventually bog the story down, but for a chapter or two, or in short story form, narrative pacing can work. We know that action and suspense must lead *somewhere*, and we can build to that somewhere deftly and successfully with narrative pacing.

It might begin with description:

> High on the mountain were two middle-aged Norwegian spruce trees, greenish-blue, sturdy and serene in thinning forest that once dominated the lives of thousands in the homes below. No one could remember how long the Norwegian spruce had been there, nor whether they had been planted or had simply sprouted mysteriously from the dense, dark earth. But they had become beacons of stability to the valley inhabitants.

Or it might begin with an anecdote:

Thirty years before Jim Plover was born, a stranger appeared in the village and asked for directions to the forest fire warden. Normally, no one thought much about this because the forest began at the village edge and swept up the mountainside into the clouds, and there was always a procession of hikers and campers coming through. But this stranger was different, he was in buckskin, and his hair flowed over his collar and down his back.

From these beginnings we slowly build the story, developing conflict that will support action and suspense. We can go on with the narrative for some time, adding events or characters or conflicts until we reach some sort of crisis or resolution, or until we decide we had better make a change in pace.

Narrative pacing works because we show what is happening; we are moving the story forward, using description, anecdotes and character development. As we depict what happens, we keep our readers involved because the story continues to unfold and the action and suspense grow taut, until we reach that crisis or turning point.

Then, perhaps, comes the change in pace. But not before.

Narrative pacing works best when:

- it opens the story or chapter.
- it will run on at least several pages.
- it builds to a crisis.
- it keeps the story moving.
- it develops conflict early and keeps it pulsing.

The narrative way. It highlights the storyteller's art.

MIXING AND MATCHING

And then there's dialogue. No writer can ignore dialogue when considering the pace of a story. It isn't that a story must include dialogue. (Take a look at Ernest Hemingway's "Big Two-Hearted River," for instance, which contains 99 percent narrative.)

But dialogue's presence or absence must be gauged for its effect on story pace. Would dialogue make the story stronger? Does the story need some beefed-up drama (which dialogue could add)? Is there so much narrative that the reader could begin to lose interest?

Questions such as these are—or should be—part of every writer's self-examination when face-to-face with an early draft or a story plan. Weaving between narrative and dialogue is a balancing skill, and clearly, there are occasions when one or the other should dominate.

Do we want drama?

> "I said to put that inkstand down!"
> "You've always hated me!"

Do we want a sense of place?

> The raw earth exhaled pungent solemnity, shrugging off the manicured firs and textured pines that offered carved-out exclusivity.

We can turn the tables, of course, because narrative can be dramatic and dialogue can offer a sense of place. But the point is that both dialogue and narrative play necessary roles in a story, and we should carefully gauge their effects on pacing when we're putting our story together. Too much of one or too little of the other, and the reader tends to suffer from that, by now, familiar malady: *boredom.*

Not always, though, as we can see from the Hemingway example. And if it's a predominance of dialogue we seek, take a look at George Higgins's novels where most everything takes place while the characters are talking with one another. Action, suspense, conflict development—these are well-portrayed by Higgins, even though there's little straight narrative.

But these are exceptions, and for most of us, mixing and matching narration and dialogue is the most comfortable way to write. We try to avoid reader *bog-down,* where the narration or the dialogue goes on and on and on until the reader's patience comes to an end.

Take a look at *Polar Star* by Martin Cruz Smith (Random House), the story of murder aboard a Russian fish factory ship in the Bering Sea, and the efforts of a discredited Russian detective to solve the crime. The book opens with two pages of narration describing the netting and disgorging of the fish catch aboard ship. Along with the catch comes the drowned body of a female crew member. The next page and a half continue narration, describing the ship, its work and the assembly-line preparation of the fish catch for the freezer spaces:

> In the course of an eight-hour watch the gutting and spraying spread a mist of blood and wet pulp over the belt, workers walkway. . . .

The next sentence describes one of the workers on the assembly line. Then, the first word of dialogue:

> "Renko!"

Followed by a half-page narrative paragraph describing Renko's work on the assembly line, and the way he coped. Then, the second line of dialogue:

> "You're Seaman Renko, aren't you?"

And soon other passages of dialogue and narration become interwoven. But the important thing to note is that narration runs for four and one-half pages before meaningful dialogue intrudes. The writer is using narration to accomplish at least two things:

- to establish early conflict, not so much between characters (though the woman's death might imply that) as between characters and the elements and the atmosphere
- to create an action sequence that will undoubtedly be built upon (the appearance of the dead woman)

Both spur the reader's interest, but if the narration continued for much longer, the immediacy of the conflict and the action would disperse because the pace would begin to lag. Immediacy is the lifeblood of drama, and the further away we get from that, the less excitement there will be for the reader. We need to keep the reader involved, and a careful mixing and matching of narration and dialogue ensures that will happen.

Heavy narration, or heavy dialogue? Martin Cruz Smith goes the other way, too. In a scene midway through the book, his protagonist speaks at length about the dead woman's past. In two and one-half pages the author produces twenty-three separate dialogue passages, ending with:

"Lenin?" Natasha perked up. "What did Lenin say about murder?"

"Nothing. But about hesitation he said, 'First action, then see what happens.' "

Then, in the next scene, Smith goes back to narration for two pages.

And now we have building suspense as the detective slowly investigates the death and the clues and the circumstances. Both dialogue and narration work with suspense, and, of course, there is the intensity brought by the conflict, too. But it wouldn't work so well if there wasn't a careful hand on the pacing throttle. With action and suspense, reader involvement and story immediacy are crucial, and the way we mix and match dialogue and narration will determine how long we hold the reader.

There are no hard-and-fast-rules about when to use narration and when to use dialogue, though we can generalize a bit: If we want to describe something happening, narration might work better (and, thus, action might be emphasized); if we want to portray emotions or feelings, dialogue might fit better (and, then, suspense might be emphasized); if we want to develop conflict, both narration and dialogue can be used.

But remember this: Action and suspense support both narration and dialogue, though one may tend to build more slowly (narration), and the other may tend to reach out more quickly (dialogue). The key is to avoid spending too much unbroken time with either one.

Pace the narration.

Pace the dialogue.

And find the reader in lockstep.

CHAPTER 12

ENDINGS

ONE DAY MY EDITOR CALLED with a request: "I've got a short novel I'd like to publish, but it's got flaws. Would you take a look?"

Over the years this editor and I had developed a mutual respect and we felt free to consult each other. He mentioned that the book was a bittersweet tale of enduring love between two elderly people. "It brought tears to my eyes," he said.

"Let's have a look," I said, and after a few pages I, too, could pick up the emotional appeal. It was a powerful story, and I could readily identify with the main characters. I read it through once, then again. As I came to the last page a second time, something caught my eye. The elderly couple was carrying out a mutual suicide pact, and their last conversation was drifting into shards of vague disconnection. Their breathing grew slower and less sustainable; their fingers, entwined in a forever grip, lost certainty and their minds began to recede from a satisfied consciousness.

The final line announced that they were no more.

What caught my eye was this last line. The ending. "I think you should remove it," I told the editor.

"I like the way it ties things up," he said.

"It's redundant," I said. "We see the elderly couple expiring, and we know the ultimate outcome. Let things drift off."

"I'll take it up with the author," he said, clearly unconvinced.

I heard nothing more about the manuscript until the editor

sent over galleys months later. "Thanks for your help," he wrote, "much appreciated. Endings can be tricky."

Naturally I turned to the final page. There! The final line was gone. The story was allowed to expire as the characters, themselves, expired. Rythmically, harmoniously.

Now it was tied up well.

A surprising number of writers have difficulty with endings because there isn't a simple mechanism they can refer to. With openings we know we've got to grab the reader's attention right away, and we explored ways to do that in chapter three. There are certain opening techniques that are practical and will work, and a writer who has been paying attention to his craft will use them. But endings are more difficult because the techniques aren't so concrete. We know, for example, that we should retain the reader's attention throughout our story and that the ending has to make sense to the reader; we know, too, that endings shouldn't be anticlimactic or confusing. They should be clear and certain and creative.

But all of this doesn't give us much on *how* we go about writing them. The techniques and the mechanisms for developing clear, certain and creative endings are more abstract and less direct than those that work with openings. Most stories depend upon a ready supply of conflict and tension, and the one thing all endings must have is the culmination of that conflict and tension. Imagine a story that climaxes with the destruction of the bad guys . . . only we still have fifty pages to read. Where can the conflict and tension go but in a downward spiral? Where can the action and suspense go but into a passive dissolve?

Those final fifty pages become relics to futility and a reminder that endings should come when the interesting part of the story is over. Not before, certainly not afterward. This means that if the final scene or scenes are action-filled (a chase, for example, or a hunt), the story should end when the action stops. It shouldn't carry over for another twenty or thirty pages explaining, characterizing, touching up and formulizing. All of this needs to be done much earlier so that the story and the ending can occur on a high note, so that readers can have most of their questions answered, so nothing dangles.

Suppose we're trying to develop suspense. As we know, un-certainty is the underlying prescription, but when we get to the ending, what happens?

Certainty replaces uncertainty, explanation clears up the inexplicable. Some things, of course, remain outside our logical realm. Think of William Peter Blatty's *The Exorcist* (Harper & Row), in which weird physical events are explained by supernat-ural occurences, and that's the way it is left. But even here some kind of explanation is offered, and it's enough to wipe away some—if not all—of the uncertainty. Think of Stephen King, whose horror tales reek of the unexplainable, yet by the end we have some certainty and explanation. The point is that while stories with suspense must live by uncertainty, they shouldn't end that way, at least not completely. Readers *must* go away satis-fied, and that means they must know more than they knew forty pages from the end. The story line cannot disintegrate before the ending, it must retain tension and conflict right to the last page.

Otherwise the impact of the action and suspense is doomed. No action, no suspense . . .

No readers.

KEEP SURPRISE AND DELIGHT COMING

It's a human thing, I suppose, to want to slow up as we approach the final paragraphs of our story. After all, when we drive a vehicle, we don't screech to a halt under a red light or slam on the brakes when entering a parking space (unless our minds are elsewhere); we slow down and gradually stop, mindful of our own comfort as well as that of our passengers. Kinetic movement of any sort, in fact, seems best controlled when it comes to a stop gradually, easily, rhythmically. No abrupt stops, no unexpected jarring.

Writing, of course, is different. A story can come to a nice, smooth, gentle stop, but it doesn't have to. We know how impor-tant conflict is, and once that conflict evaporates, the story—any story—tends to wither. Since conflict is the bedrock of action and suspense, as we noted in chapter one, we'll want to maintain that conflict as long as we can, if we want our story to have impact.

A story that glides to an end (such as a memoir or gentle character study) wouldn't work for readers seeking high drama and excitement because the conflict would be dampened. And readers have a right to expect the writer to keep them interested right down to the last line. As I mentioned earlier, don't make the mistake of underestimating readers' expectations; they *know* the kind of book they are reading, they picked it up because it promised action or suspense, and the writer better deliver!

Gliding to the finish line isn't for them. They want that abrupt stop, that slam-on-the-brakes:

> "Villains!" I shrieked, "dissemble no more! I admit the deed! — tear up the planks! — here, here! — it is the beating of his hideous heart!"

These are the final lines of Edgar Allan Poe's "The Tell-Tale Heart." In these last lines the murderer finally succumbs to psychological pressure and admits his murder. That's all; the story ends right there.

Poe has kept the surprise and the delight (the reader's, that is, not the character's) coming; he hasn't stopped short or reduced his dramatic impact. The murderer admits his guilt. *Bang!* It's over. Action and suspense to the last line.

Certain stories lend themselves to endings such as this:

- fingering of (or admission by) a murderer
- discovery of a long-sought treasure or solution
- final destruction of a character or relationship
- final cementing of relationship or power

Note these carefully: Each relies on conflict and tension for dramatic impact (that is, there should be conflict and tension in the final lines), provided we *stop* at the appropriate time. Take the final destruction of a relationship, for example. These could be the last lines:

Father and son glared at one another through the hard iron bars. A lifetime rolled into these few seconds before the curtain fell.

"Luck," Jimmy said, moving away.

"Shove it," grunted Big Ed, "you're nothin'."

More suspense than action here because we don't know until these final lines whether the relationship will be saved. But the suspense rides along until the uncertainty becomes certain — father and son will not be reconciled.

Could we make it action-oriented? Change the locale to the deep woods, father and son hunting for deer. Son disrupts father's shot and announces he is an animal-rights activist. Father shoots him in the leg and stalks away, telling him to call his animal friends to help him survive.

Here's action, spurred by conflict, changing the focus but not the type of ending. Do we really need to know more? Will the son survive? Will he come after the father? If we've built our story well, we don't need to answer these questions. The relationship, itself, will have been fleshed out to the point where this ending is appropriate. If the reader can be satisfied, then we as writers should be, as well.

Because we have that partnership with the reader. As in any partnership, we take comfort — and pleasure — in knowing that each of us leans on the other for overall success.

The way our story ends is the final impression we leave with the reader!

Does the reader come away excited and satisfied? Or bored and irritated?

The decision is yours.

QUESTIONS AND CHOICES

Remember those themes and compositions we used to write in school, and how our teachers would insist that nothing be left unresolved?

"You introduce a thought here, then you let it dangle."
"You don't tell us what's to become of the characters."
"You leave us in the dark."

We've all been faced with a variation of these criticisms, and for the most part they are useful. We *should* tie things up, we *should* avoid unanswered questions, we *should* allow the reader to understand what has happened.

Endings that keep the reader in the dark or prevent a story resolution are not effective. For one thing, the reader will go away unsatisfied, and we know how that will influence this reader's attitude toward the writer. Unmet expectations carry a long grudge.

Shakespeare is always a good example of how things should be tied up: Look at *Hamlet, Macbeth, Julius Caesar*; there isn't a major unresolved question left for the reader to ponder. In each work we know the identity of the conspirators, their motivations, their targets, and their plans once they acquire power. We know why the most tragic figures (in order: Hamlet, Macbeth and Brutus) join the conspiracies and then fall victim to the forces they have unleashed. And we know what befalls the major characters as the conspiracies play themselves out.

All major questions answered, each ending carefully tied.

Is this the way every story should be handled? It certainly makes for symmetry, but perhaps story writing should be less geometric. All of us would agree there should be discipline and control in a story; things should happen logically and progressively, and matters should proceed to a satisfying conclusion. But does that mean every question must be answered? Can we leave nothing on the table?

Our primary interest must be the reader. However we end our story, the reader must not feel cheated. If it's a murder mystery, for example, and we fail to identify the murderer, the reader won't be pleased. After all, we embarked on the story, bargaining with the reader—come along as we seek to solve this crime, we'll make it interesting, exciting. What we didn't do was add a caveat: *Expectations may not be met!*

So, when the ending doesn't settle things, the reader has a right to complain.

Occasionally, though, endings don't have to work this way. Questions can be left, choices don't have to be made. The story can proceed to where the major issues have worked themselves out, but new challenges might arise. Is it necessary to resolve *every* uncertainty in the interest of story symmetry? Must we become slaves to a neat, tied-up story package?

Take a look at Frank R. Stockton's classic "The Lady or the Tiger." Two doors face the prisoner, and he must choose: Behind one is a beautiful woman and freedom, behind the other is a tiger that will maul him to death. He gets but one choice. Normally, the writer would resolve the dilemma, and the story would end. But Stockton does it differently, and that's why this is a classic: *He doesn't resolve the dilemma!* The story ends as the prisoner reaches to open one of the doors, having received a signal from his beloved who knows which of the doors conceals the tiger and which conceals the beautiful woman. Does his beloved steer him to certain death because she can't bear to lose him to another, or does she put aside her personal happiness so that he might live?

The single question—life or death—remains unanswered. "And so I leave it with all of you," writes the author with his last sentence. "Which came out of the opened door—the lady, or the tiger?"

Does the reader feel cheated? The fact is the two-door dilemma becomes a new challenge, not for the characters (who were aware of it from the beginning), but for the reader who never saw it coming. And the reader can understand that the bargain made with the writer at the beginning has been fulfilled because by the end of the story the only item that dangles is whether the young man lives or dies. Readers see this as a challenge, not as an unmet expectation because the author never led them to expect anything else. This is, after all, only a story, and, as with reality, matters aren't always packaged perfectly. Readers don't expect miracles—only respect.

Action and suspense key into this well. War stories, for example, such as Norman Mailer's *The Naked and the Dead* (Rinehart) or Michael Herr's *Dispatches* (Knopf), leave unanswered questions at the end: How will the survivors cope with civilian life, will the heroes and the cowards continue to be remembered, who bears the greatest scars? If the authors tried to answer these new challenges, still other issues would emerge, and the stories would be never-ending.

What about suspense? Here's an excellent vehicle for ending a story with new challenges. Suspense equals uncertainty, and every new, unresolved challenge presents uncertainty. Just as Frank Stockton offered choices to his protagonist in "The Lady and the Tiger," we can do the same. Then . . . *end*.

Suppose a member of the Irish Republican Army is on the run for crimes he committed years before. He yearns for his estranged wife and twelve-year-old son, and he sneaks quick visits with them from time to time. But mostly he's hiding and running. Now suppose the authorities are closing in, even as his wife is helping him to elude them. He becomes trapped in a wooded area and continues to resist.

This is *The Trigger Man* by Joe Joyce (Norton), a mixture of action and suspense that moves to the final page. The suspense is palpable: Will he elude the authorities and continue to survive as he has for such a long time? Will the relationship with his wife blossom once again?

Alas, the uncertainties fall apart as he is destroyed in his wooded enclave. His wife is arrested and will be sent to jail. But the new challenge is his twelve-year-old son. What will happen to him now? This was not a challenge until the final pages, but it shouldn't leave us dissatisfied. The reason? It's a *new* challenge, not something that has hung over the characters chapter after chapter. The boy had been safe with his mother through the years. Suddenly, the net is gone. What will happen to him?

The author doesn't tell us, but that's all right. It's a new challenge, a new question.

Old challenges we should resolve. But new challenges?

Let the reader ponder them.

REACH FOR THE CLIMAX

Take this as the nearest thing to an unbreakable rule: *Where action and suspense predominate in a story, the climax must come at the end, preferably on the last page but certainly in the final chapter.*

Think of a delicately made birthday cake, freshly baked, thick with gooey icing. Suppose the cake is ready three days before the birthday party, and the host and hostess decide to send pieces to the guests ahead of time. "It won't stay fresh," they say. "Enjoy it now." Three days later, at the party, the host and hostess announce: "Pretend we bring out the cake, pretend we cut it and eat it . . . pretend we enjoy it."

"Pretend we're having a good time," one of the guests murmurs.

"What's a birthday without a cake?" another complains.

"I'm bored," says a third.

Replace birthday cake with story climax, and you have the reason for putting the climax at the end. "What's a birthday without a cake?" one of the characters complains, and what's meant is as simple and straightforward as an editor or writing teacher asking, "What's a story without touch-and-go to the end, without a final climax?"

Whether it's a birthday party or a story, the climax cannot emerge so far in advance of the party or story end that it loses significance. A cake that's eaten ahead of time has little, if any, impact on the birthday celebration three days hence; a climax that comes twenty to thirty pages from the story end provides little impetus for the story to continue (or for the reader to keep reading). All the good stuff—the important stuff—has been devoured too early, and what we're left with is an anticlimax.

Which is nothing more than a writer playing out the string or the story sinking slowly beneath the waves.

A key ingredient is the level of tension you wish to maintain. Normally, stories *build*, developing more intense confrontation and drama as the story goes along. When the climax comes, tension should be deep and widespread and excruciating (think of Stephen King's endings and the explosive suspense that comes in the final few pages; it is something he consciously builds toward). The tension level will determine the impact of the climax — the greater the tension, the more dramatic the climax. Think of Shakespeare's *Othello* where the climax comes in the final scene as Othello discovers he has been duped by Iago into believing his wife, Desdemona, was unfaithful. Because he has killed her in a rash of jealousy, he now takes his own life. The drama level, at this point, is extremely high: Othello is at war with himself (because of guilt over killing Desdemona) and with Iago and the other conspirators (who are unmasked as his enemies). His world is in shambles, and his only recourse is to destroy himself.

Such high conflict produces dramatic climax, and that's the case here: a realization of wrongful murder, an awareness of trusted friends who are really enemies and ultimate self-destruction, all in the final scene. And because he knew the value of reaching for this climax, Shakespeare allows but five spoken passages to follow Othello's fatal act. Then it's *The End*. He does not dilute its impact.

Here's the way it's done:

- Make the climax the hottest action scene (or the most intense suspense scene).
- Rev up the conflict (turn up the emotional heat, zero in on the deadliest enemies).
- Leave the final confrontation to the last scene, if possible (the last page would be even better).
- Stay away from injecting sudden new elements such as a new plot line or new characters or a new setting; stay with what has taken you this far (because readers expect it!).

We "reach" for the climax when we preserve it to the end of the story and build toward it. We'll want events to grow in significance as the story moves along. More people should become involved, more important consequences should develop, more dangerous happenings should occur, until the climax when all of these things come together, and the impending drama makes the reader hang on every sentence.

Or we'll want uncertainties to grow as the danger to the characters compounds. Answering one question only creates another question where the answer becomes more elusive. Finally, we come to the climax, and here the level of suspense and danger has become excruciating, and as the climax plays out, we resolve, at least partly, the festering uncertainties. Suspense grows as the story moves along, but the highest level of suspense should be left to the climax. That's where it will do the most good.

Take a look at Alistair MacLean's *Ice Station Zebra* (Doubleday), a story resonating with action and suspense set in the coldest part of the Cold War. It's about an American nuclear submarine and a British meteorological detachment in trouble on a polar ice cap. The submarine is dispatched to rescue the British, and by story's end there have been eight murders, a fire on the sub, explosions and general mayhem. Two chapters from the end, the narrator (posing as the ship's doctor but actually a British agent) calls eleven people together in the submarine wardroom and explains how and why much of the violence has occurred. The chapter ends with:

> "It seems too superfluous to add," I said, adding it all the same, "that the murderer is in this room now."

In the final two chapters, the narrator goes through step-by-step analysis of identifying the murderer, and three pages from the end, there is confrontation between the narrator and the murderer, with the narrator prevailing, of course. Then, four paragraphs from the end, there is this:

> Mouthing soundless words through smashed lips, his face masked in madness, and completely oblivious to the two guns, Jolly flung himself at me. He had taken two steps and two only when Rawlings' gun caught him, not lightly, on the side of the head.

A half page later the book ends, and the reader is satisfied because there are no major questions left unanswered—the identity of the murderer, the reasons for the murders, the ultimate fate of the murderer are provided . . . and it all comes at the end. The final confrontation (by far the most intense one in the book) begins three pages from the end, the conflict pulsates (because we're talking life and death), and the final confrontation ends on the last page.

That's the way to wrap things up!

BACK TO THE BEGINNING?

We've read about—and perhaps have seen—people in public who find it difficult to finish what they've started and exit the stage or give up the microphone. On and on they meander, seeking that go-away line or triumphant flourish. Finally, in desperation, they'll sigh, mumble about taking up too much time and walk away uncomfortably.

And how much of what they offered will be remembered? Not much, of course, because we, the audience, would be feeling their discomfort more than listening to their words.

Endings like this sometimes plague writers. A slow dissipation of thought and drama, spiraling downward to oblivion, losing readers along the way. As we've seen, one way to prevent it is to place the major climax at the end of the story, and another is to provide the reader with a new challenge on the final pages. Action and suspense demand this—keep the reader's attention focused even as the story perks to an end, keep those surprises and delights coming without interruption, and the reader won't sense any awkwardness.

But at some point we do have to end the story, and action and suspense require the same control as any other literary creation. Essentially, there are two ways to finish stories, and both will protect us from hemming and hawing as we search for the proper exit lines:

- *Circular endings*: where the story comes to an end at the same or similar place it began
- *Linear endings*: where the story moves steadily forward

reaching a climax far removed from where it began

Each ending seems to work best with different types of stories:

- If the story seeks a soft landing, the circular ending would be better. Returning the story line to where it began is like fitting one end of hose into another; it slides together smoothly, softly, easily, creating an unbroken whole and a satisfied reader.
- If the story builds and builds to an exciting, shattering climax, the linear ending would be better. Both action and suspense work well here because something must be happening (action) and/or uncertainties must grow and grow . . . until the climax brings one or both to a head.

Note the differences between these types of endings: The circular ending

- concentrates on contrasts of then/now, before/after, showing changes that have occurred in attitude, place and position.
- usually has characters returning to or rediscovering the original story setting.
- can tie up loose ends after the climax (as long as it doesn't go on and on).
- ends not with a bang but with a whoosh!

The linear ending

- shows characters and plot to have developed beyond original portrayal.
- stops *right after* the climax (the loose ends should already be tied).
- introduces no new characters, settings or subplots.
- should be the result of a story narrowed to its essential conflict/confrontation, its "ultimate" struggle.

How do these endings work? Let's look at Isak Dinesen's *Out of Africa* (Random House) where a young married woman and her husband settle in Kenya in the 1930s, buying a farm and working it. This is a suspense tale, in part, because the author's survival and her peace of mind are rarely secure. The opening sentence reads:

I had a farm in Africa, at the foot of the Ngong Hills. The Equator runs across these highlands.

Eight years later, after increasing tragedy and unhappiness, the farm is sold. On the last page the author is standing on the railroad platform, leaving the area forever. The first sentence of the final paragraph goes:

From there, to the South-West, I saw the Ngong Hills. The noble wave of the mountain rose above the surrounding peaks.

Here is a circular ending: The author begins by describing the farm in the Ngong Hills and ends by taking her leave of the Ngong Hills. She has brought the story full circle, and she has done it quietly, smoothly. The climax actually occurred when she decided to sell the farm and leave (this was the major conflict—should she or shouldn't she sell the farm?). But the *leave-taking* is an important part of the book because it ties up beginning and end, and with circular endings, we don't worry so much about anticlimaxes. It's more important that everything should come together smartly.

There are many examples of linear endings: The novels of John MacDonald and his fictional detective, Travis McGee, are among the best. Most stories begin with McGee on his houseboat and end with him returning there, but the endings are linear, nevertheless, because the stories have built up to a major climax only a page or two from the end. McGee's returning to his houseboat will change the ending to a circular one *only* if the item or person who started him off on the mystery is there for him to settle with. Then, the story ends with a resolution of the problem at the place where it was created. But McGee generally works things out at a place and with people at a distance from his houseboat, so the ending really is linear.

What difference does it make? If we can label the kind of ending we wish to create, then we know what the demands of that ending will be. If it's circular, we'll want a soft, smooth ending without explosive fireworks and much action; if it's linear, we can go ahead with the fireworks and build to an action-filled climax, knowing we don't have to bring things all the way back to the beginning.

All of this doesn't mean we have to decide what kind of ending we want before we even write our story; what it *does* mean, however, is that we should understand which kind of story works best with which kind of ending:

> If suspense is our game,
> circular's the only name . . .
> If action's where we turn,
> linear's what we learn . . .
> And when we come to conflict,
> our talents won't be so tricked
> Because now we know the measure
> of a generous writer's treasure.

Isn't this an ending you'll remember?

And doesn't it put things back where we began?

Conflict, action and suspense. Openings to endings and everything else between.

In partnership with our readers.

INDEX

More of the Best From Writer's Digest Books!

Snoopy's Guide to the Writing Life—*Snoopy's Guide to the Writing Life* presents more than 180 heartwarming and hilarious Snoopy "at the typewriter" comic strips by Charles M. Schulz, paired with 32 delightful essays from a who's who of famous writers, including Sue Grafton, Fannie Flagg, Elmore Leonard and more. These pieces examine the joys and realities of the writing life, from finding ideas to creating characters.
ISBN 1-58297-194-3, hardcover, 192 pages, #10856-K

The Pocket Muse—Here's the key to finding inspiration when and where you want it. With hundreds of thought-provoking prompts, exercises and illustrations, it immediately helps you to get started writing, overcome writer's block, develop a writing habit, think more creatively, master style, revision and other elements of the craft.
ISBN 1-58297-142-0, hardcover, 256 pages, #10806-K

The Writer's Idea Book—This is the guide writers reach for time after time to jump start their creativity and develop ideas. Four distinctive sections, each geared toward a different stage of writing, offer dozens of unique approaches to "freeing the muse." In all, you'll find more than 400 idea-generating prompts guaranteed to get your writing started on the right foot, or back on track!
ISBN 1-58297-179-X, paperback, 272 pages, #10841-K

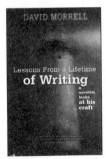

Lessons From a Lifetime of Writing—Best-selling author David Morrell distills more than 30 years of writing and publishing experience into this single masterwork of advice and instruction. A rare and intriguing mix of memoir and writer's workshop, *Lessons* pulls no punches. Morrell examines everything from motivation and focus to the building blocks of good fiction: plot, character, dialogue, description and more.
ISBN 1-58297-143-9, hardcover, 256 pages, #10808-K

These books and other fine Writer's Digest titles are available from your local bookstore, online supplier or by calling 1-800-448-0915.